T0265520

Portrait of Phillipe le Beau
c. 1490

Paris in Winter

Paris in Winter

AN ILLUSTRATED MEMOIR

DAVID COGGINS

pH powerHouse Books Brooklyn, NY

To Wendy, David, and Sarah

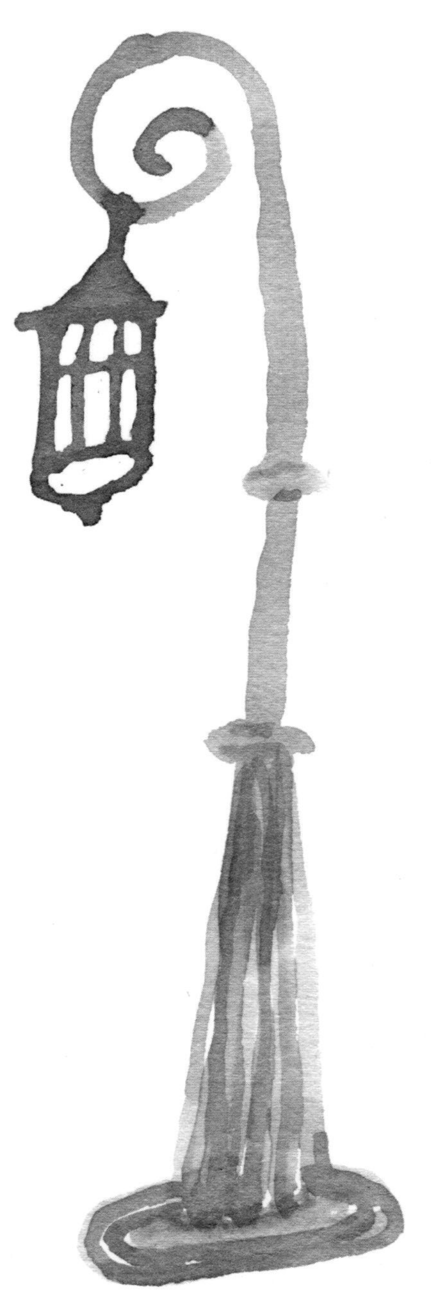

Paris in Winter

THE YEARS

INTRODUCTION

It's winter, we're back in Paris. We are standing with Jacques and Adeline outside Céleste, the bar atop the Hôtel Cheval Blanc, on a brisk January night. "We've never seen Paris like this before," I say. "From on high at night."

"It is rather extraordinary," Jacques says. "The hotel just opened. Everyone is coming up here."

The panorama is stunning. Your eye follows the Seine from Notre-Dame in the east to the Eiffel Tower in the west. It takes in the tall steeple of Sainte-Chapelle, the glowing domes of the Panthéon, the Institute of France, and the Hôtel des Invalides. Below are Pont Neuf, the city's oldest bridge, and Pont des Arts, the popular pedestrian bridge that leads to the Louvre.

The river heaves with the wakes of barges and *les bateaux mouches*. Lights from street lamps, apartments, cars and motorcycles glow and flicker. It's breathtakingly beautiful. It reminds us that there is always something new to discover in Paris. Ancient Paris continues to change and surprise.

We no longer come *en famille*. Wendy and I still come for extended stays, but David and Sarah are here less regularly and for less time. They come with their amours, roam the city on their own. We do make the rounds together to favorite cafés and restaurants, shops and gardens, the latest exhibitions. Our history here is deep, our paths well-worn and well-loved. There is still plenty of the old city to enjoy. Paris remains our family's place, a comforting retreat in a troubled world.

We talk about changes. The burning of Notre-Dame, the arrival of Uber, the transformation of dark intimate shops into soulless modern rooms. Of more strikes, of outer *arrondissements* growing more desperate, of tourists, driven by social media, swarming at every turn, of summers turning hotter, of Covid.

There are new museums: Bourse de Commerce, Hôtel de la Marine, the Giacometti Institute. Fondation Louis Vuitton in the Bois de Boulogne still seems new. This year, inside Frank Gehry's flamboyant sailboat of a building, is a vast exhibition devoted to the work of Mark Rothko.

A number of new illustrations appear in this edition (the second) of *Paris in Winter*. This introduction is also new, but the chapters remain the same. I am deeply grateful to the many who have written or posted to say they've found pleasure in the book. It gives me hope that it will continue to find new readers just as Paris finds new devotees.

We say goodbye to Jacques and Adeline and cross the Pont des Arts to the Left Bank. We pause on the bridge to take in the Eiffel Tower, its lights sparkling madly as the hour turns. "It never gets old," Wendy says.

"True," I say, "but we do."

"No, Paris keeps us young."

1997

The Paris table at New Year's is an epicure's delight, and a test of endurance. I order a bottle of red wine for our table of three at Guy Savoy. "And for the white?" the waiter asks as if it's a matter of course to have one of each. The long evening starts with a plate of lentils and Périgord truffles and ends with grapefruit terrine, tea ice cream, and a slice of apple tart. In between is marmite of duck, pheasant, and foie gras served in a coal black pot whose lid, sealed with crust, is cut away in front of us.

A Polish magician makes Wendy's ring disappear and at midnight a cart rolls through the room bearing bottles of champagne in a silver bowl and a large cake pierced with fizzing sparklers. Spoons banged on copper pots and shouts of "*bonne année, bonne année*" tell us 1997 is here.

We arrived in Paris after a few days in snowy Burgundy. We drove on the sleet-streaked autoroute with broken windshield wipers, pulling over to clean the windows or relying on splashes from trucks.

"We made it," Wendy says as we lift our flutes.

"Well done, my wicked and depraved colonel," David says and clinks my glass. (I had been reading, in sleepless nights at the château, Hemingway's *Across the River and into the Trees*. "A ridiculous book," David says.)

"Bonne année," I say. "Here's to Sarah. Is she in Houston or New Orleans?"

In the lobby of the Montalembert, three Japanese men tipsy in party hats serenade the night porter. David and I, smoking cigars, wave at the amusing trio as they stumble up the marble staircase. Wendy says cigar smoke makes her feel green and heads for the elevator. It's four in the morning.

Legend has it the painting that started it all is called *Impression, Sunrise.* It hangs in the Musée Marmottan, a converted hunting lodge in the outlying 16th. It was part of an exhibition in 1874 by a group of artists calling themselves *"La Société anonyme des peintres, sculpteurs, et graveurs, etc."* Louis Leroy, a painter and a critic of the time, didn't like the "slapdash" work and in a review contemptuously called the artists "impressionists" of mess and sloppiness. The name stuck, and so, of course, did the work of the anonymous pretenders – Degas, Renoir, Pissarro, among them.

The trek out to the Marmottan to see Monet's iconic painting (though very far from his best work) is de rigueur for students of art history. Photos of the great man are also on view. The image of the pasha strolling Giverny gardens in suit, straw hat, and bushy beard is almost as well known as his paintings. Monet's sun is still rising.

Our room has yellow and white striped walls, dark Biedermeier furniture, and a view of the Eiffel Tower across the rooftops. The bed is too short for a tall jetlagged American.

The thick duvet and *Some Like it Hot* take our minds off the nippy streets of Saint-Germain-des-Prés.

In one small bohemian place, a wine-soaked man at the bar yells over his scarf, the size of a horse collar, at some poor waif who, lingering at the door, lets in a dart of cold. *"La porte!"*

The more crowded the cafés the better. More bodies, more heat. Scarves, wrapped and tied like sailors' knots, are not removed even in front of espresso. Smoking is rampant. Parisians must think the burning of cigarettes provides heat. There seems to be more style in winter. There is more to wear: fedoras, sleek coats, sexy sweaters, beautiful leather boots, the scarves. Endless layering of wool, silk, denim.

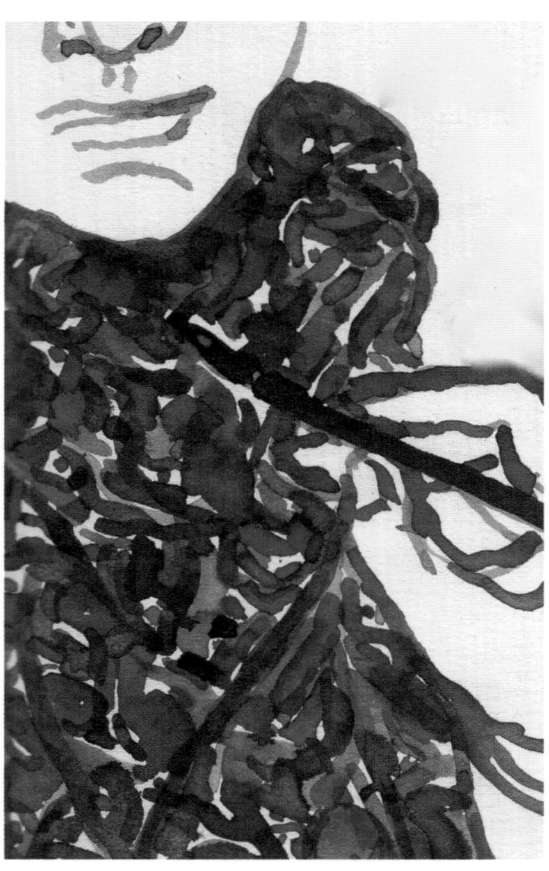

SOLDES
le bulldog
Fur Coats
Rue du Bac

Palais Royal

Food is better in winter if not fresher. You have more of an appetite. Not to mention its warming power. Hot wine with cinammon at Le Petit Saint Benoit goes right to the bone. So does old-fashioned *céleri rémoulade* and *blanquette de veau*. Everything about the creaky bistro, at least the icy day we are there, warms the spirit; from the blood-red sign, to the stubborn old revolving door, to the woman writing down our orders on the paper table cloth.

Le Voltaire also offers shelter from the storm. Let it snow. We sit in a paneled room with soft light, chicken and lamb on the table. Next to us are entertaining Italians and across the room small dogs politely wait their turn to eat. The waiters are witty. This is our first time in this classic river bistro.

We go into an antique shop on rue de Beaune as much to thaw out as to admire the warm patina of a 16th-century chest from Bologna. A bookseller on rue de Seine offers us champagne when we step into his shop. Candles burn in the windows. He tells us the owner of the hotel across the street just died on vacation in the Caribbean. "He drank all the day."

Wendy's favorite paintings in the Louvre's Great Hall are Leonardo's portrait of a woman (*La Belle Ferronièrre*), Cimabue's *Madonna with Child,* and Fra Angelico's *Ange en adoration.* I like Jules Romain's portrait of Jeanne d'Aragon and della Francesca's *Sigismondo Malatesta.* Pisanello's *Portrait d'une jenne princesse de la maison d'Este* is also on the list. "She has so much columbine around her head," Wendy says.

"What is columbine a symbol for? You majored in art history."

"I'm sure it's in that book I love, *Signs and Symbols in Christian Art.*"

"*Colombe* is French for dove."

"Let's say it's a symbol for peace."

In the Musée d'Orsay precious Degas pastels line a small dark room. We are permitted to see them only by means of *"une faible luminosité."* Manet's single lemon is as enchanting as anything in the museum. In an odd but charming touch, the austere museum offers visitors suffering impressionism fatigue gray wicker chairs, like those on Midwestern porches.

The lives of Proust and Madame de Sévigné seem entwined like vines. Both wrote about aristocratic life. Her 17th-century letters were part of Proust's 20th-century novel. The beautiful marquise lived for twenty years in the Hôtel Carnavalet long before it became the city museum of Paris. His cork-lined bedroom, where in his last sickly years he closed himself off to write, has been recreated in the museum. Perhaps the two eloquent Parisians are less like tangled vines than like the spiraling hedges in the Carnavalet gardens, the evergreen arabesques curving inward like time itself.

Winter and fatigue catch up with us. Wendy and David are under the weather. Our last night we eat in the hotel. The waiter recommends rum for a cold and Badoit "for the conscience." "What do you recommend with the langoustine ravioli?" I ask. I feel fine and tomorrow it's home to real winter.

Over the public address system at Charles de Gaulle: "Someone left a sombrero in the terminal. Please come forward to claim it."

1999

Sarah arrives from New York, joining the three of us who spent New Year's at Château de Courcelles, near Reims, drinking champagne. "You brought warm weather," Wendy says.

"I always follow the sun," Sarah says.

"You are the sun," I say to her.

"You follow the brother," David says.

La Hune is handy to the cafés in Saint-Germain-des-Prés and it's open late. The bookstore is a place to go for a shot of cosmopolitanism after a shot of brandy. We usually find ourselves there on one of our first nights in Paris. The low-ceilinged second floor has an extraordinary selection of art and photography books. Pouring over them at midnight is a treat, like staying up late to watch a movie. Inside one book are letters written by Manet embellished with fruits and flowers in his quick masterful hand.

A sign at Reid Hall in Montparnasse, where David studied while in college: "American writer working in Paris looking for young writers to forge a literary movement."

The sun shines on the newly scrubbed face of Notre-Dame and on the smiling faces crossing bridges to and from Île Saint-Louis. Spring-like blue sky softens the bare branches in Jardin du Luxembourg. Children in poetic sweaters push sailboats and ride ponies. The green chairs around the pond and many of the benches in the gardens are full. So are the tennis courts and the carousel. There are shrieks from soccer games, murmuring in the *allées,* laughter across the *boules* lanes. It is a world at leisure, at play as if May.

We have lunch on a glassed-in terrace. Fish as white as a waiter's apron is presented before taken to the grill. A price tag is pulled from the gill of a sole. Sarah, newly twenty and not a fish lover, says, "I wanted a sandwich."

"You are mother and daughter *magnifique,*" the maître d' says.

David, moved by the wine perhaps, finds a phone in the basement of the restaurant and calls Yuko in Tokyo. He is spending his first year out of college teaching in Japan. "She is celebrating New Year's with her family in salt baths by the sea. They eat a tremendous amount of fish."

David orders *les cervelles d'agneau* at Le Voltaire, forgetting or probably not knowing what *les cervelles* are. He is an adventurous eater but not that adventurous. "Is this what I think it is?" he asks, looking pale and lambish. Embarrassed, he asks if the dish can be replaced. He orders *les côtes d'agneau.*

"You started with the head of the lamb and then went to the leg," the waiter says when he brings the new plate.

David writes "*merci*" in *frites* on his plate.

As we are leaving, someone in the restaurant asks him if he is an actor. "*Oui,*" I say, "*il est Monsieur Cervelles d'Agneau.*"

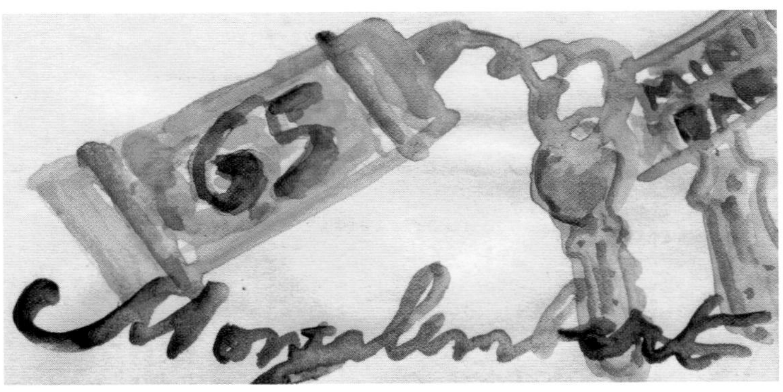

David + Sarah
Hotel Montalembert

Paris is made for strollers. After dinner, David and I walk for a couple of hours with no destination in mind, going where our feet take us. We cross the river and walk through the quiet Tuileries to Place de la Concorde. From the big square, we see to the southwest the 1000-foot colossus of lacy pig iron known as the Eiffel Tower (loathed by Maupassant, loved by Cocteau), and more westerly the Champs-Élysées and the Arc de Triomphe in Christmas glitter. Then up rue Royale to La Madeleine, a Paris church that looks like a Roman temple.

The city is magical at night. The streets and squares, many of them deserted, are gracefully and generously lit for nocturnal wanderers. Historic buildings and landmarks are also aglow.

"Damn it, lad," I say, "it sends chills down your spine."

We do a little window-shopping on rue Saint-Honoré and circle the obelisk in Place Vendôme. The square is lovely after dark. It would make a great outdoor ballroom. People could dance to a Chopin mazurka, minding the cobblestones of course. Chopin died in an apartment on the square before he turned forty.

We pass by the Comédie-Française, then cross rue de Rivoli and stop for a moment by the ethereal pyramid in the Louvre's Cour Napoléon. The ten-year-old structure is almost as much a fixture in Paris as the Eiffel Tower. We cross the river on Pont du Carrousel to Quai Voltaire and head back into the Left Bank.

Wendy calls them "the little green paintings."

The group of wonderful portraits by Corneille de Lyon are on the second floor of the Richelieu wing in the Louvre. Born in the Hague in the 16th century, de Lyon settled in France where he became painter and valet (shifting between canvas and closet) to Henry II. The portraits are small and mounted in ornate oversized architectural frames. The faces are painted with sensitivity, but what's also striking are the solid backgrounds in glowing olive green and sky blue. One especially touching is of a poet with sad, piercing dark eyes and dark wispy beard.

Red, especially dark red, is a color I associate with Paris. It's the color of wine, of rare beef, of radishes, of lips and nails, of love. It's the color of décor, of plush curtains and chairs. Think of the burgundy interiors of the Paris Opera in the Palais Garnier or the Comédie-Française. And the arabesque crimson love seats in the salon of Napoleon III or the banquettes in Le Grand Véfour.

It's the color of blood, of power, of art, of passion. Heads rolling on cobblestones, the robes of kings and cardinals, Matisse's *The Red Studio,* the red in the tricolor flag of *Liberty Leading the People* by Delacroix. The red hot jazz of Stéphane Grappelli and Django Reinhardt, the red sizzle of Bardot, the red balloon.

At the Fondation Cartier is an exhibit of Issey Miyake's brilliant designs, which have as much to do with engineering and technology as they do with fashion. Miyake creates ways to make garments from one piece of cloth, even from one piece of thread.

Later in the Louvre sculpture galleries, we stop at the *Winged Victory of Samothrace.* A lot of it has been restored (including all of the right wing), but the folds of the draped cloak are astonishing. "The sculptors were like Miyake," Sarah says. "They made their figures out of one thing, one piece of marble."

"Miyake made permanent pleats, the sculptors made permanent drapery," I say. "Well, sort of permanent. Even marble crumbles."

We may prefer the paintings of Watteau and Chardin in the plainer galleries of Sully to the huge 19th-century history paintings in the Denon wing, but Denon with its herringbone floors and richly painted walls is more reminiscent of the old palace. Delacroix's tigers and scenes of North Africa, Corot's wistful, silvery landscapes, Courbet's nudes and portraits, the sensuous precision of Ingres. These I gravitate to. But nothing beats Watteau's *fêtes champêtres* or Chardin's still lifes.

The Goncourt brothers called Jean-Honoré Fragonard "the divine cherubino of erotic painting." A darling of the old regime, Fragonard is frivolous and licentious, but more often he is light-hearted and intimate. And the brushwork is dazzling. Yesterday at the Louvre we stood before Fragonard's portraits and boudoir scenes, today we sit at Fragonard's table in Le Grand Véfour. "Fragonard died a poor man in the Palais Royal," the waiter informs us. The restaurant began life around the turn of the 18th century at the time of Fragonard's death. Both represent a hedonism and love of life that one hopes will never go out of style.

At the end of an alley off the tiny rue de Vichy in the 15th, Le Cirque Tzigane Romanès pitches a blue tent by a bunch of trailers. A man in a black hat lets you inside after taking your francs and putting them in a box. Inside incense burns. Two gypsy families, kids to grandparents, put on the show.

A dark-haired beauty walks with a cat across a tightrope just feet above the ground. A bald man juggles, girls dance and contort, boys do flips. The man in the black hat coaxes a goat up a ladder. A woman wearing a bright skirt sings brassy gypsy songs. A small band plays just behind the performers, who when not jumping around, sit in a row of chairs with the musicians. There is an accordion and a violin, a clarinet and drums. Everyone on and off stage claps.

"No lions, no tigers," the ringleader says. It's whimsical and funny and irreverent, an anti-circus circus. It could take place in a large living room. After the show, sausage and beignets and beer and wine appear on "the stage" and people come down from the bleachers.

The man's moustache twitches slightly as he pierces the beetle with a thin black pin. Next to it in the box is another beetle and a butterfly. He holds the box up to show us the arrangement. Butterflies and beetles from far-flung jungles, sizes pea to pear, colors boot-black, celadon green, tomato red, lie in rows behind glass. On the way to *Entomologie* we pass an elephant, a tiger, a giraffe, and a zebra all standing about as if at a cocktail party. A stunning menagerie of exotic birds stares at us from their perches without blinking. Wandering the creaky wooden floors of Deyrolle, on rue du Bac, is a lot safer than setting up camp on the banks of the Amazon, and almost as interesting.

Slabs of foie gras are served by short, thick waiters. A crisp whole-roasted chicken and grilled *côte de boeuf,* the size of a football, come with a hillock of *frites.* The bistro, with a dozen dark tables, grows smaller as people eat and drink and talk. The heat from the wood stove makes the place all the more primal and garrulous.

"Have you ever seen Rubens' cycle of portraits of Marie de' Medici?" David asks. "There are twenty-four of them."

"I have a headache," Sarah says.

"Is it the sight of all this food?" I ask. "Or the thought of all those portraits?"

She asks the waiter to get her coat down from the rack, where it was cavalierly tossed half an hour earlier. She puts it on and disappears into the rainy night.

How many museums in Paris are dedicated to artists? There's the Picasso, the Rodin, the Delacroix. Musée Maillol on rue de Grenelle is another, and along with the brawny nudes of Maillol, it puts on exhibits almost always worth seeing. Up this winter are paintings by three London heavyweights – Francis Bacon, Lucian Freud, and Frank Auerbach. I like Auerbach's worked and reworked canvasses of thickly layered oils, from which a face or a street emerge. He paints only people and places he knows well and spends a lot of time looking at paintings in the National Gallery. "Painting is a cultured activity," he once said. "It's not like spitting, one can't kid oneself."

Thé à la menthe drops like a miniature waterfall into our cups. The waiter in Au Pied de Chameau pours from the teapot with precision. Having worked our way through most of the piquant Moroccan dishes, the pink sheen of having eaten well colors our faces.

"You look like a soccer coach in that sweater, Dad," David says.

My glow starts to fade, just as it did after lunch, when Sarah lectured me on being grouchy. "Life is not seamless, Dad," she said. "There are problems and irritations. You deal with them. You can't always complain." A man may feel like a king in a foreign land, but not among his family.

The antique shop is full of globes and ships. I pick up a tiny ball of wood on a wooden stand. It's no bigger than an orange, yet wrapped around it on segments of painted paper, like slices of the orange, is the world. Seas and continents are almost impossible to make out because the colors have turned with time to blackened yellows and greens. Through a magnifying glass, I can see Lisbon, London, Paris. In North America the names of a few states.

This little copy of the earth, dark and unreadable, has incredible power. Despite its size, it makes the world seem big. It undermines the notion of a shrunken world. It somehow plays a trick on the mind. To travel back and forth as we moderns do from city to faraway city is so easy, like Little Leaguers tossing a baseball back and forth. Airport to airport, glove to glove. It may be easier than it once was, but it's still a miracle. Like the ball thumps when it hits your mitt, your heart thumps when the plane touches down in Paris.

Champagne circulates in our suite of rooms as we pack. "Do you think the *sablés* will make it back without crumbling?" I ask.

"We can't eat them all before we leave," Wendy says, holding up the large bag of Poilâne cookies purchased earlier in the day. "We'll split them up."

"You probably still have some in the freezer from last year," Sarah says. "Or five years ago."

"*L'amour dans le coin,*" Sarah says about the young couple cooing like doves in the booth at the restaurant.

"Isn't that the title of a film noir?"

"*La mort dans le coin,*" David says.

Duck with olives, chicken with potatoes, Pommard, a humorless waiter who makes us laugh. On the dark deserted rue de l'Université we find ourselves singing and skipping and clicking our heels. Tomorrow we go our separate ways, David to Berlin, Sarah to New York, Wendy and I to Amsterdam. Tonight, for one last night, we are in Paris.

2000

To Paris for the millenium. Einstein is the man of the century. Everybody is worried about the Y2K bug. Wheels up at 3:40 p.m. After endless dark sea, the lights of Glasgow.

The storm of the century has struck northern Europe. An estimated seventy thousand trees are down in Bois de Boulogne and Bois de Vincennes. Trees on the banks of the Seine are under racing brown water. Damage is put at five billion dollars. There is nothing to do but drink the champagne waiting for us in our room and take a nap under the black and white duvet.

"Le Maroc de Matisse" is drawing big crowds at the Insitut du Monde Arabe. Lucky for us because we are going to Morocco after Paris. *L'Arbre de vie,* from the Vatican, is two long colorful panels of *papier collé* leaves, bringing to mind the chapel at Vence. *Zorah sur la Terrasse* is a painting of a kneeling Moroccan woman, brilliant *babouches* and bowl of goldfish at her side. There is a photograph of the plump Matisse in a tunic.

At dinner in the paneled "club car" of Le Voltaire, Christian Lacroix knocks over an Evian bottle as he passes our table. "*Il est vide?*" he apologizes. "It is empty?"

Wendy, radiant in green silk blouse, sips the Marc offered at the end of the long meal. "You sold your flower business," I say. "Now you can travel the world."

"You can travel the world. I have to look after the dog and the house."

Three steps from bed is a view across violet night sky of the Eiffel Tower, the color of rust. It is as familiar as a water tower in a country town or the elm tree in your backyard. Its shape is eternal. The Eiffel Tower is something I have always known.

New Year's Eve: a shot glass of caviar, crème fraîche, and vodka. "*Il continue,*" the waiter says as he sets down roasted capon. He says this each time another in the parade of plates is served. Each time more dryly.

We rush from the restaurant to the river just before midnight. People are everywhere, running along the river, crowding the bridges, singing, kissing, hoisting bottles of champagne, tossing fireworks. The air is electric, alive with joyous *bonne années* and crazed noise-making. A black-tie party looks down from a balcony. The Champs Élysées is a sea of delirium. A dozen Ferris wheels along the boulevard spin slowly, like many-handed faces of time. The sky to the west is green. Fireworks explode near the Eiffel Tower.

From our balcony we look out at the tower sparkling like a rocket of diamonds. Brilliant white lights race up and down. On television, we watch the celebration spread across the globe – Sydney, Moscow, Berlin, London. The world for a moment is one big happy family.

In the first hurrahs of the year 2000, three million people dance in the streets of New York, including Sarah Windmiller Coggins. "An amazing time to be alive," she says over the phone.

Four a.m. Out the window the Eiffel Tower sparkles madly as if trying to speak. "Go bravely into the new century."

Christmas a week ago. Walking in fresh snow, dinners with Barbra and Charlie and Julie, playing tennis with David, Christmas Eve soufflé, grilling on the snowy deck, Wendy's much promised *dobos torte,* the languorous morning opening presents around the fire with Bella's head on Sarah's lap, the lacy tree, choral music, blues mixed with Arabic

chant, football games, garden in winter, wide lurid sunsets, sleepless nights thinking of Paris, where I am now not sleeping.

From our balcony we can see bells swinging in the belfry of Église Saint-Thomas-d'Aquin. The ringing is beautiful and loud. It's the first day of the new millennium.

A French couple sits by the lobby fire with a bottle of champagne and a large jar of caviar. In the rue de Buci market, across from the red-scarfed oyster shucker, a broad-chested man with chinchilla hair fills the air with bel canto arias.

Yeltsin resigns, hijackers release passengers on an Air India plane, endless talk of the "wide-band" era.

Thirty-three tons of garbage is collected in Times Square after the New Year's celebration.

Sixty-four percent of Americans did not vote in 1998, fifty-one percent in 1996. The first times since 1924 a majority did not go to the polls.

"Crimes against humanity will be the litmus test of the 21st century," CNN forecasts.

"A time of promise and peril," says one pundit.

Le nouveau siècle.

Morocco is also at the Musée Delacroix on Place de Furstenberg. Delacroix's watercolors of interiors and baggy pants, of medina and Tangier *plage* are fresh and delicate. Baudelaire called Delacroix, who died in 1863, the last of the great Renaissance artists and the first modern one. The museum is the artist's former home and studio. You can poke around his library, his bedroom, even his garden. One huge wall in the studio is all windows. On a table are palettes with dabs of hardened paint, the colors still strong.

A young man in a wheat-colored linen suit hands me the bag, a black tin, and a Japanese scoop. The tea is a Darjeeling SFTGOP1 – special finest tippy golden orange pekoe (second flush).

"Tea expels heavy dreams, cures constipation, vanquishes dullness, eliminates fear, and reinforces intelligence," wrote Cornelis Bontekoe, a 17th-century Dutch doctor, in a treatise called "Tea, that Excellent Beverage." Maybe I'll drink tea more often. I would like to have my intelligence reinforced and my dullness vanquished.

It's lunchtime. People eat oysters alfresco at a restaurant near l'Ecole des Beaux-Arts. Tall green heaters warm the chilled air. We order a platter of oysters, keeping our vow to eat lightly. Then *côte de boeuf,* breaking the vow. Then a bottle of old Bordeaux to help us forget the vow, like sinners at confession.

A satiny golden retriever lies on newspapers by a woman in a pillbox hat. "Of course, the dog is well-behaved in public. She's British."

din
"un
nouveau

Morning.

Rue Montalembert. A terrier squats on the sidewalk in front of the hotel. Holding the dog's leash is a man dressed in a suede jacket and wool fedora. In one swift, shameless moment he soccer kicks the little orange *bonbon* into the gutter.

The owner of a shop in the Marais sings about Morocco. "You will love it," she croons. *J'aime Marrakesh.* You will love it. *J'aime Tangier.* You will love it."

She sounds like Edith Piaf.

Noon.

Oulah, a black mutt with a pointed French nose, sits in the front seat of the taxi. The driver gives Oulah a biscuit. "She rides around all day listening to jazz."

Amid the young philosophers lunching in Les Philosophes, a craggy Bostonian speaks a guttural, unintelligible French. Not just a few words, whole sentences. I guess they are sentences. I can't make out a thing, but I can't stop listening to him. It's as if he is making it up, like a comic Marlon Brando.

Night.

Lobby of the Montalembert. An American with a giant Brillo pad for hair takes Franglais to new heights. He is trying to sell his house in Tangier to a Frenchman (shirt unbuttoned to sternum) and his silent, sultry girlfriend. "*Ma maison est* out of this world," the American exclaims. "*Extraordinaire. La vue est magnifique.* All the way to *Espagne.* Across the blue sea *quand le ciel est clair.* Clear. Blue. *Bleu. La mer est* blue. *Bleu.* Like your eyes."

Champs de Mars. The Eiffel Tower shines down on a scarlet red motorbike pulling up in front of an elegant apartment building. A man in a scarlet red Pizza Hut uniform and helmet gets off the motorbike, pizza in his upturned waiter's hand, and rings the bell.

The earth will lose over half its animal and plant life in the 21st century through destruction of rain forest. "The sixth extinction." CNN again. Advances in stem-cell research will lead to the replacement of body parts, making it possible to create a person from scratch. An expert gives Americans a poor grade for not being able to enjoy leisure or engage in self-reflection.

"You don't have that problem," Wendy says to me. "You get an A."

2001

David and Sarah take the Eurostar from London and switch from a room reeking of cigarettes at the Lutetia, to a room above us at the Montalembert. David talks about having after-hours champagne with Laura at Gagosian, the new reading room at the British Museum, the new Tate. Sarah brings Christmas presents from New York.

At midnight the lights go out in the bistro. There is low-key cheering and polite kissing. "This is not the way we celebrate New Year's in Brazil," says a dark-haired young man sitting with his pretty girlfriend.

An American man lifts his glass to the Brazilian and says, "Dance on the tables, man. Don't let us stop you."

David and Sarah go to a party in a Place Vendôme apartment rented by an American actor. The star's chef, a woman from L.A., tells Sarah that her brother has beautiful eyes.

At the Musée d'Orsay is a show of the exquisite still lifes Manet painted as he was dying. The dark, fluid flowers, the oysters, the lemon. He painted a single spear of asparagus as a gift for a collector who paid too much for Manet's painting of a bunch of asparagus.

The museum's Belle Époque dining room with its painted ceilings, chandeliers, and big arched windows is as fresh as the year it was created. It was the dining room of the Hôtel d'Orsay, built in 1900, along with the train station that is now the museum.

"I love the big vases of flowers," says Wendy, the flower artist. "They must spend a fortune of francs."

Jean-François sits down at our table at La Palette. He invites us to dinner in his new apartment. The bearded, brusquish owner of the café befriended David when he was a student in Paris. They played tennis on Sunday mornings. Jean-François would drive his big Mercedes and pick him up on the Place de l'Opéra. "He wore black socks and brought a dozen croissants, which we ate during changeovers."

The giant Ferris wheel next to Place de la Concorde is blinding up close, its lights like white-hot rhinestones. The square, the largest in Paris, was the site of less innocent activity during the French Revolution. The square's name was changed from Place Louis XV to Place de la Révolution. A guillotine replaced the statue of the king and, like the Ferris wheel, had a lot of customers. During the Reign of Terror, "the nation's razor" (as the Michelin calls it) fell on over thirteen hundred heads, including most famously, those of Louis XVI and Marie Antoinette. Now an ancient Egyptian obelisk flanked by fountains dominates the center of the square. Cars and people are thick in the streets. The blood of history has long washed away.

We start in the Richelieu wing – the French wing – where some of my favorite paintings reside: Watteau's *fêtes galantes* and his wonderful sad-eyed Gilles. Chardin's serene still lifes and time-freezing portraits. We race through Poussin, linger a long while before Corot, Delacroix, and Ingres. We all love the *The 1821 Derby at Epsom* by Géricault, the horses flying, not galloping, through space. And there is the wall of Daubigny's moody woodscapes.

Café Marly is suffused with gray winter light. The Napoleonic room of black wainscoting and maroon walls overlooks the Louvre pyramid. It's a modern restaurant with style, something the French are not always good at. It's a place where the setting and the people you are with are more important than what you are eating. Food plays second fiddle for a change.

I order a nice bottle of white Burgundy. The waiter still wet behind the ears suggests that I take a sip of water before tasting the wine. "To prepare the palette," he says helpfully.

A handsome, fiftyish man parks a vintage green Rolls Royce outside the hotel. As he checks in, he strokes the backside of the statuesque woman beside him.

Not everyone has a mobile. A man in a phone booth on rue du Bac talks loudly while staring at a map of Paris. He holds the map like a palette, pierced by his thumb.

Le Bistrot Mazarin in the 6th is open on New Year's Day, a godsend for travelers and claustrophobes. We have dinner with Brad and Wade, who spent Christmas in the Dordogne, helping a friend renovate an old farmhouse. The oysterman comes in from the cold followed by an African selling toys.

"My wife is a *contessa*," says a man at the next table. He addresses us, then the room. "She is beautiful, no?" He has a booming voice and is a little tight. The lavishly dressed *contessa* buys several wind-up toys. She sets off a tiny airplane and a gyrating woman on the tables for everyone to see.

"She's a *contessa. C'est vrai.*" The man laughs loudly. We all laugh. Smoke fills the air. Wine spills. "Beautiful, no? *Qu'est-ce que vous pensez?*"

"My wife is a duchess," I say. "The Duchess of Kenwood."

The man looks at Wendy. "Beautiful," he says and laughs. "Beautiful."

in

"My daughter doesn't know what she's missing," Wendy says after she orders the pheasant with *foie gras*. The breasts are cut at table, from the center of the bird, held upright on a board. Sarah, professing fatigue, is in the hotel room eating *pasta nature* and watching *High Sierra*.

"Did you know there are only twelve da Vinci paintings?" David says.

A Japanese man eating alone takes pictures of his plate while the vivacious French woman at the table next to him feeds her lap dog bits of *poulet*.

Back in the room with Sarah, we gather around Humphrey Bogart and Ida Lupino on the small screen.

"I'm tellin' it to you straight."

"You stinkin' rat."

"They are *mauvais* types, aren't they?" Wendy says.

Sometime in the 18th century Prosper Mérimée, the author of *Carmen,* came upon something astonishing in a castle: a woman seducing a unicorn. Not in flesh, but in thread, elegantly woven in the 15th century by Flemish artisans to a French design. The six tapestries were installed in the Hôtel de Cluny, once a home for monks built over Roman baths, that is now the city's repository for medieval marvels.

La Dame à la Licorne tapestries hang in their own room in the museum. The reds, greens, and golds are still rich and strong. In each, lady and unicorn are joined on an Edenic isle of flowers and trees by a lion (the unicorn's comrade), servants, pennants, and an attractive array of rabbits, monkeys, and birds. Five of the tapestries are devoted to the senses. One features an organ, another a monkey smelling a rose.

The seduction is conjecture, but mythology has it that the unicorn risks relinquishing strength and power to be with a virgin. In the "sight" tapestry, the unicorn, its paws perched coyly on mademoiselle's lap, looks into a mirror.

If you don't get your fill of romance in the museum, you can stroll in the gardens outside. Jardin d'Amour and Forêt de la Licorne. Or, on the slightly less romantic side, a kitchen garden and a garden of medicinal herbs. And for what comes after romance, a children's playground.

Parisians love their museums and their gardens. Start with art, the main course, and for dessert a stroll in the park. The museum at Jardin du Luxembourg is crowded today. A hundred pieces from a German's collection have been assembled under the enticing title "Fra Angelico to Bonnard." The ancient floorboards groan under winter boots. You squeeze past shoulders and hips to stand before a canvas, if only for a few moments.

The garden is lively too, even in winter. Young men in scarves hit top spins, old men toss boules through cigarette smoke, chess players in plaid jackets sit and stare. The pony carts are busy and families line up outside the puppet theater. We walk to the apiary as we always do and look at the hives now dormant and the bees painted in gold paint on the pale green post.

If you want to see paintings without crowds go to Église Saint-Sulpice, a short walk from Jardin du Luxembourg. Big Delacroixs are on the walls and you can gaze at them undisturbed. The only problem is you can't see them in the dark church.

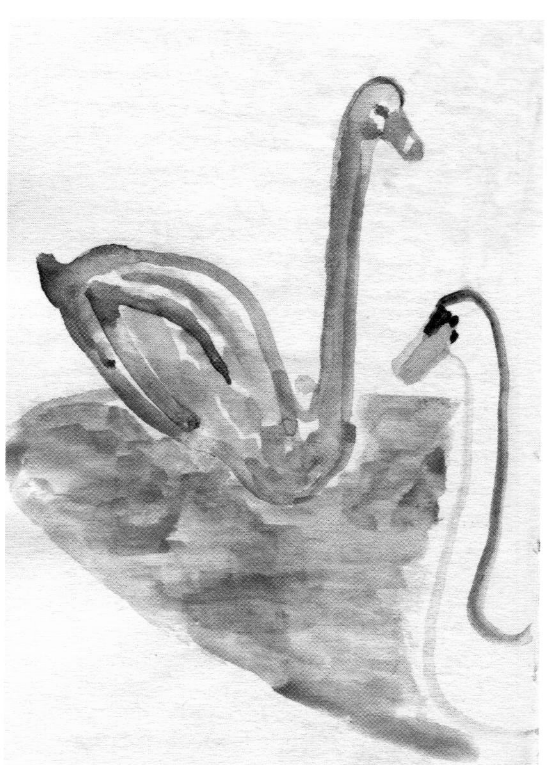

Sarah at the Ritz

Except for a Texan who speaks fluent French, the four of us are the only people in the tiny restaurant, a once famous bistro on rue de Fleurus, owned by an elderly couple. We order lamb and wild duck from the mimeographed menu and a reasonable 1976 Bordeaux that arrives with no label. *Madame,* an earth mother with few teeth, pours it without pretense into a heavy ornate pitcher. After the meal, *Monsieur,* the well-fed chef, comes to the table in white toque and apron and checkered pants.

"*Je suis vrai français,*" he says merrily. "*Je suis un grand Camembert.*" He raises pigs and lambs and says the best meat in America is in California because "*les vaches mangent* the wildflowers." He cooks only what is in season. He tells Wendy how to make veal stock. His son, who lives in Connecticut, "*est un vrai Américain.*"

He pretends to throw and hit a baseball in a way not even Buster Keaton could have dreamt up. Straightening his toque, he says he got a speeding ticket driving from his village to Paris. "*Deux cent kilometres* by hour." His hands are on a mock driving wheel.

All the while, *Madame* is in the kitchen beating egg whites for soufflés. I can hear the whisk against the metal bowl.

"Is this your first time at the Ritz, Mr. Coggins?"

The porter holds open the gate to the round, oak-paneled elevator. Up we glide. Inside a small entry are three doors to a suite of rooms, each with a doorbell, each opened with a blue plastic key. Barbara Hutton arrived with seventy trunks, we with but a few.

"The hall smells of perfume," Wendy says.

"*Eau de Ritz,*" David says. The smell, we learn, is for sale. A prominent catalog on a table in the sitting room displays pictures and prices of everything Ritz: the Ritz bathrobe, the Ritz tissue box, the Ritz coasters, Eau de Ritz.

Pale silk walls, heavy curtains, tapestries, fireplaces, scrolled woodwork, padded doors. Bathrooms are marble with silver swan faucets and porcelain pulls in the tub marked MAID and VALET. A sign in the WC informs us that if we are paying by check we must tell the hotel four days in advance.

Flicking one of the light switches (shaped like violin stops), the real world falls away. All is cushioned, soft, muffled. From the small balcony is a view of a garden, a bit of the Eiffel Tower, and the tip of the column in Place Vendôme. We hear the sound of children's voices. We think of our old neighborhood across the river.

"You look like a Fabergé egg," David says to his mother bundled in a thick peach bathrobe. The underground pool is small and shallow and has an air of Roman decadence with its painted walls and ceiling and swaddled men and women napping or drinking tea. A gentle Asian woman twice shows me the way out of this dreamy cavern.

I meet David at the Ritz barbershop while Wendy and Sarah visit the coiffeur. A quiet Russian pulls his straight razor easily across my chin. It's my first time. David, oft-shaved, says, "It's the best thing in the world." The coquettish assistant wraps my new skin in a hot towel and massages it sensuously with warm oil.

Sarah, her curly hair now straight and flowing, flies around the suite like Ginger Rogers. David promenades in towel and Speedo goggles. We drink the complimentary champagne as we dress for dinner.

A smiling Monsieur Vrinat ushers us into his warm and gracious restaurant. Like the Ritz, Taillevent is about providing a buffer. The headwaiter is named Yann. He takes us smoothly through the truffle-laden menu. We put up little resistance. Wendy: a green salad covered completely with thin shingles of truffle; tiny lamb chops and grilled artichoke and fennel. Sarah: poached eggs in a shell with truffle cream and parmesan toasts. David: mashed potatoes with truffle; veal. Me: a whole truffle with *foie gras* and spinach in a crust covered with *sauce Périgreux;* pigeon.

"David, how can you eat a baby cow?"

"With caramel sauce."

"Here's to the best revenge," I say. "Eating well."

"Here's to the last revenge," David says. "Gout."

In the Hemingway Bar a French woman with black zigzag stockings and thick, black glasses smokes thin, colored cigarettes. Her laugh sounds like a cough. Currants float in glasses of water. David lights a cigar. Colin Field, the Ritz's illustrious barman, pours Cognac. At midnight we circle the haunting, austere Place Vendôme. Like an owl, Napoleon keeps watch atop the column in the middle of this square of classical architecture and million-dollar watches. The bed in the Ritz is a cloud.

Wendy and I have breakfast in L'Espadon (The Swordfish), the hotel's restaurant. Waiters in tuxes move about like stagehands beneath painted ceiling and swaths of curtains. A woman hooks her purse on the pickled branch of her chair. A man resembling Robert De Niro in old age drinks glass after glass of grapefruit juice. He demands a baguette and fiddles with his unlit cigar. *"Pas de* cornflakes today, *Monsieur?"* the waiter asks.

George W. Bush is inaugurated. Stains have appeared on the titanium skin of the Guggenheim Museum in Bilbao. Cricket and Fred Rogers on television. Arab and Indian channels. The world's poor number six hundred eighty million.

Rue Saint-Honoré in the rain. "I am wearing my Left Bank shoes on the Right Bank," Wendy says. A saddle in Hermès is several thousand dollars. Two Japanese women, shopping bags swinging, run like rabbits in front of a herd of cars on rue de Rivoli. A man turns chestnuts, roasting in a pan, in deep silence as if meditating. Puddles cover the red clay soil of the Tuileries.

At lunch, Wendy listens in on two genteel American couples. One of the women says, "They have great sex. Can you believe it? It gets better and better. It's his fourth wife."

David and Sarah go to the Marais. Wendy and I take the Métro. "I don't like the Métro," Wendy says. "I can't see the city." We surface on the other side of the river in the 6th. In an antique shop on rue Jacob we meet Gilles, the proprietor. "France is beautiful," he says, "but more and more people are too interested in money."

"I love your French tulips," Wendy says. "Do you call them French tulips?"

"J'adore les perroquets. Ils sont beaux."

Didier, a former food broker, now dealer in art and antiques, has a shop on rue de l'Université and a home in Cap d'Antibes. "You could visit but it is flooded at the moment." He lifts open the top of a large 17th-century table made of fruitwood. It's called a *petrin.* Under the top is a trough for kneading pasta dough. "The French are contemplative," he says perhaps by way of salesmanship. "Americans are decisive."

After dinner we cross back over the river under the waning moon. The Ferris wheel circles slowly at the end of the Tuileries. We cross rue de Rivoli and walk down rue de la Paix to Place Vendôme. "*Bon soir,*" says the Ritz doorman.

We order drinks in the bar and talk about romanticizing the past. "When you look back at the Belle Époque...," I say.

"You can't live in the past, Dad," Sarah interrupts. "What about cell phones? What about rock and roll? What about leisure suits?"

Tomorrow David goes to New York, Sarah to

Amsterdam and Prague. Wendy and I are headed to Barcelona. In the hotel, ridiculous and grand, we lift glasses in gratitude and remembrance of things passing.

2002

Coast out. Coast in. Rain in Amsterdam, rain in Paris, but warm. A Belmondo driver with a passion for churches. Fifteen hours door-to-door without a hitch. Only jetlag and a wracking cough.

"Have a good nap," Sylvie says.

Dinner by the river, cognac in the café. Scarves, cigarettes, bookstores, little dogs. Churchbells, umbrellas, water in gutters. The sound of French.

Historic Paris, is it a fantasy? A gold-leafed Disney World?

Museums are like churches. At least old Paris museums. The light is dim, floors throw back footsteps, and the air is rarified if warmer. Most people go to museums and churches for the same reason – to be uplifted, to be comforted.

Looking at Raphael portraits in Musée du Luxembourg has a feeling of sacredness about it. We follow a satisfying ritual as we go from painting to painting, studying the face, the dress, the skin, the words on the card. We smile at the feet of the unicorn, between the thumb and forefinger of the blond maiden in *La Dame à la Licorne.* Note the thumb of homely *La fornarina* (was she Raphael's mistress?) holding a piece of gauze between her breasts.

Raphael's famous portrait of the 16th-century diplomat Baldassare Castiglione has come across the river from the Louvre. Castiglione in his rich gray and black velvets is a gentleman of grace and restraint. Can one tell from his gentle eyes and air of kindness that he was a master of *sprezzatura?*

Sprezzatura, Castiglione tells us in his book on the courtier, is the studied nonchalance that "conceals all art and makes whatever one does or says appear to be without effort, almost without thought." For Castiglione, and other men of culture and manners seeking favor in the courts of the Renaissance, light touch and heavy discretion were required. Raphael and Castiglione were friends and traveled in the same elevated circles. That the noble and humane courtier appears to have effortlessly materialized on canvas in such a winning way shows the painter was not lacking in *sprezzatura* himself.

People dodge puddles in the Tuileries and sit in the Sunday sun drinking coffee under the leafless trees. The giant Ferris wheel spins in the cold blue sky, on its side a sign reading *"Ensemble contra la SIDA."*

"Do you want to go for a ride?" I ask Wendy.

"Too cold, too high, and too fast."

"What about the view from up there?"

"I like Paris on the ground just fine." She wraps a second scarf around her head.

"A two-scarf day?"

"I may look like a peasant but I'm warm."

We leave the *allées* of plane trees, go around the Ferris wheel, and cross the vast Place de la Concorde. We follow the long curve of the river to the Musée d'Art Moderne, where hang at the moment the paintings of Giorgio Morandi. The Italian painter, in making mystical art out of simple bottles and pots, reminds me of Chardin. A boy lies on the floor copying one of Morandi's paintings in his notebook. Completely engrossed, he is unaware of the people pausing to look down at his drawing.

The Eiffel Tower is getting painted. I read that it takes over fifty tons of paint, brushed on every seven years, to keep the latticework looking up to snuff. People wait in long lines for the thrill of seeing Paris from on high. Hundreds of millions have done the same in the century or so since the tower was built. Eiffel thought it would stay up only twenty years. Hitler ordered it destroyed. De Gaulle wanted to move it to Montreal.

la pluie
RES
ART

Two handsome men discuss their New Year's plans at the café, over plates of eggs. Under their table bags of Veuve Clicquot and vodka. One is German and excited. He orders, over his cell phone, clothes from Yves Saint Laurent. They have just come from the shop and he has made up his mind. "Yes, yes, the white patinated jacket," he stutters. "And I want the shoes, the beige shoes."

"Cognac," his friend says. "The color is cognac."

Two a.m. Johnny Walker in a champagne glass. Where is sleep? In Sebald's *The Emigrants*?

> *That evening, a hundredweight of apples, goldings and red calvilles, are laid down for winter on the floor of the next room. Their scent puts me to a more peaceful sleep than I have known for a long time...*

Maybe apples are better than Scotch. The classical music station is FM 101.15, this I know. And the color of the night sky. Gray tinged with violet.

The trunks of the trees along the Seine are underwater, not a happy sight. But newly scrubbed Notre-Dame rises pale and clean in the sunlight above the crowd. The bright facades of the grand houses on the *quais* are a balm after the shadows of narrow neighborhood streets. The river, a ribbon of brightness, refreshes. On rue de Buci the young brave the cold and lift glasses at alfresco tables. Tomorrow the flag of 2002 unfurls.

A man in a tuxedo roams the marbled room, and when asked, snaps pictures of guests with their digital cameras. His only task this New Year's Eve is to press the shutter. His many colleagues, in the precise choreography of a grand restaurant, pirouette briskly beneath high ceilings and brilliant chandeliers, setting caviar broth and citrused turbot on the tables of the elegant celebrants. A diamond butterfly rests on the breast of one grand dame.

At midnight, lights are lowered and confetti is tossed. A band plays above the paper horns. Diners from nearby tables rise to shake our hands and wish us *bonne année.* Through the window, sprays of fireworks explode silently above the square. A woman poses seductively for the camera while her husband shouts "*Hola! Hola!*" into a phone. In the hall a young African girl in a short dress dances with a gentleman of the old guard.

I give the loo attendant a ten-franc note and a chocolate euro, and we step into the singing night.

The euro is here, shiny coins and bland bills, bringing confusion and nostalgia for the old familiar Cézanne notes, the Saint-Exupéry, the Debussy, the Delacroix. A waiter plucks the coins from my open palm. "We will get used to it," he says. "We have to. Will Europe be more united? I don't think so. Europe is over three hundred million people."

At night, flags of the Euro countries flutter in Las Vegas lights on the Pont Neuf. The symbol for the new euro – € – shines on the side of the bridge. What happens to the millions and millions of franc notes? What will the banks do with all of them when they are traded in? Are they doomed to extinction, like the snow leopard. What if the Euro, as the waiter implies, doesn't work out in say ten or fifteen years?

"Why is it the 'cigar-smoking' booth?" Wendy asks Monsieur Vrinat at Taillevent.

"It has a *ventilateur,*" he says.

From the *foie gras* with quince compote to the soufflé with pear cream sauce, from the champagne to the Muscat, all is perfect. Even the waiter. He has big ears and a smile to match.

"Remember when we first came here?" I say. "We ate in the lobby."

"It isn't the lobby. It's the anteroom. We were young."

"It was your fortieth birthday."

"Now you are more...how do you say?"

"Old and gray?"

"Distingué."

David arrives on a child-crying express from Zurich, where he was visiting an old friend from art school. Dinner at Le Voltaire. "Zurich is pretty," he says. "Everything is so designed, the pressure to be perfect would be too much after a while." A fetching Russian belle at the next table makes eyes at him throughout the meal. They set up a rendezvous.

"Very Russian," I say.

"Very French," Wendy says.

Sarah arrives with the usual drama. Her flight left New York two hours late and she had to dash to catch the plane from Amsterdam to Paris. The plane sat on the runway at Charles de Gaulle because of a bomb threat in the terminal. Her bags did not make it. She is in good cheer nonetheless, pretty and buoyant in a red wool hat.

Slogging through Centre Pompidou can be enervating, like slogging through biennials. In one gallery though we come upon an engaging exhibition on the work of French architect Jean Nouvel.

Nouvel designed the Fondation Cartier and Institut du Monde Arabe and has been chosen to design the new Guthrie Theater in Minneapolis. Models and photographs show buildings of outlandish shapes and inventive surfaces. A skyscraper going up in Barcelona is the shape of a bullet (or a dildo) and its luminous skin will provide light shows at night.

SOLDES

Sarah in Chanel hat

David in wool cap on way to get a shave

Architecture has been the new black in the art world for a while. We go to see new museums with more eagerness than we go to see the art inside the museums. And now we go to see exhibitions on architects' designs.

One of the world's greatest works of art is always on display at the Pompidou. Not the building or what's in the building. It's the city of Paris, visible from Georges, the restaurant on the top floor. Renzo Piano and Richard Rogers got this right. Views spread in almost every direction. Through the wall-to-wall windows, the Eiffel Tower, Sacré-Coeur, mansard roofs, chimneys pots, and other bits of beloved Paris pop up beneath the blue and pink skies and wispy gray clouds.

One thing not visible is the Pompidou.

Paris is packed with bookstores and stationery shops. On one block of rue du Pont Louis-Philippe are three or four stationery stores. The notebooks that I draw and write in when traveling are sold at Mélodies Graphiques. This shop also sells the inks of J. Herbin, which have been flowing since 1670, including a black made especially for Victor Hugo. They come in elegant bottles and have names like Cacao du Brésil or Ambre de Birmanie.

Across the street from Mélodies Graphiques is Papier Plus. I have filled many dozens of this stationer's smartly colored albums with travel photographs. Often on a winter's night at home I will take one or two from the shelf, and slowly paging through them, find us in Paris five or ten years ago meandering through the same neighborhoods we do now. Our path through the city deepens and broadens each winter and each year's album reflects that. They certainly show us getting older.

Understanding and affection grow over time. One's love for a place ages as old wood furniture ages. It grows not dull but richer. It acquires patina.

"Maybe I don't need to get albums this year."

"You say that every year."

Île Saint-Louis at dusk.

Three butchers whack at hunks of beef and pork for a crowd, pressing at the counter. David and I watch from the sidewalk. Bresse chickens, head and feet attached, clutter the window along with thick red sausages and piles of offal. In a *fromagerie* a man and a woman in white aprons press giant knives down on wheels of Camembert and Mimolette. Little rounds of goat cheese are in demand. There is a queue out the door.

I can't help going into a slip of a store, dark with books. It's called Librairie Ulysse and specializes in travel books. I find, of all things, an old Penguin thesaurus with a cleverly designed, nicely mellowed cover. A wizened but kind woman prefers francs to euros.

Later I look to see if Parisian is in the thesaurus. It's not; I didn't think it would be. What word could stand in for Parisian? Elegant, fashionable, sophisticated, haughty? If you said, "That's so Parisian," it would probably call to mind all these words, these clichés, or others – romantic, witty, contentious, food-loving – but none would suffice entirely. There is no one word for Parisian, but if I were forced to come up with one I would choose artful. Maybe I would choose Castiglione's word: *sprezzatura,* or *sprezzaturaesque.*

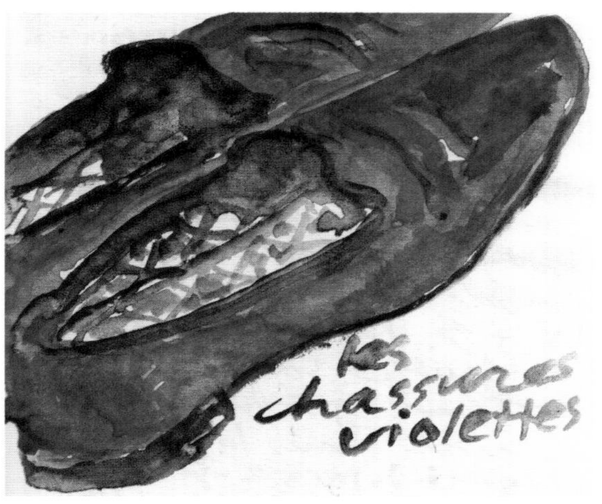

"*Les objets anciens* are my passion," says the handsome, sleepy-eyed man in the antique store. We admire a small mirror with a gold frame. "Italian, 17th-century. I am very conservative about restoration. I learn from books and from observation. I studied agronomy in school."

"Agronomy?"

"Velvet slippers and baroque mirror all in one day," Wendy says.

"Velvet slippers?" The man smiles at Wendy. "Did you buy. . .?"

"He did. Purple."

"What's the dog's name? I ask, changing the subject.

"Rimbaud."

The dog lying by the front door lifts its head and looks at us with dark, sad eyes. It yawns widely, then runs a pink tongue along its muzzle.

Sarah stops in the gallery at a white marble sculpture of a woman lying on her back. It's Cleopatra in death, having been bitten by a snake. "I wrote a paper about this," Sarah says. "She committed suicide after Antony died. She might have been poisoned."

"Why did you write about Cleopatra?"

"She was a strong and beautiful woman."

"Keep away from snakes."

"Don't worry."

Brad and Wade are stylish and funny and good company. They join the four of us for dinner in a bright restaurant in the 7th.

"You're so thin," Wade says to Sarah.

"She's just a wisp," I say.

"Dad, I'm 119 pounds."

Leaving the restaurant we are stunned by the sight of the Eiffel Tower at the end of the block. Standing there like a shimmering rocket, it is immense and otherworldly.

"Wow," Wendy says. "Why didn't we see that when we came in?"

"It just landed from outer space," Brad says.

"It makes me want to dance," Sarah says. She glides down the sidewalk dipping her arms spread like wings.

A first-edition copy of Brillat-Savarin's famous book, *The Physiology of Taste,* is on display in an exhibition called "The Art of Eating in the 19th Century." The book was first published in 1825. I remember browsing through a modern translation of the book some years ago. It begins with a list of Brillat-Savarin's aphorisms.

> *The pleasures of the table belong to all times and all ages, to every country and every day; they go hand in hand with all our other pleasures, outlast them, and remain to console us for their loss.*

From the "Odds and Ends" section there is this:

> *"Counselor," said an old marquise of the Faubourg Saint-Germain one day, speaking from one end of the table to the other, "which do you prefer, Burgundy or claret?"*
>
> *"Madame," replied the magistrate in druidic tones, "that is a case in which I enjoy examining the evidence so much that I invariably postpone judgment for a week."*

Other cookbooks are on display, as are menus and place settings, including a long table of Christofle dishes and silverware. A film of a child's birthday party (circa 1900) shows a family skittering and laughing in a black and white garden. A facsimile of the old Café Riche on Boulevard des Italiens provokes instant nostalgia.

There is a small painting of a piece of beef by Gustave Caillebotte. Known for his works of urban and domestic scenes, Caillebotte, one of my favorite painters, also made paintings of food. A wealthy man, he collected the works of his fellow painters, like Pissarro, Monet, and Degas. He gave up painting to return to the family's country estate where he built boats, collected stamps, and grew orchids.

The latticework windows, a high-tech takeoff on *moucharabieh,* animate the south wall of the Institut du Monde Arabe. Designed to control light by opening and closing like a camera's aperture, the windows (and the design of the building itself) pay homage to Arab culture. The existence of IMA, a Nouvel building, is a miracle.

On view is a collection of 8th-century Syrian artifacts. The textiles, pots, glassware, and carved wood are powerful emblems of an ancient civilization. Is it restorative, even hopeful, spending time in the museum? Yes, of course it is. When thinking about the problems of the world, one welcomes any ray of light. Often the ray is a work of art.

Rue
du
Bac

"Please allow me," says Hubert, the headwaiter. He butters the brioche carefully. He tells Sarah to dip it into the soup. "*Trempez le brioche dans la soupe.*"

"That's like going barefooted in a ball gown," Wendy says. This downhome touch makes the elegant soup of artichoke and truffle all the more savory.

The *poulet de Bresse* is presented at table in a foil pouch. A young woman cuts open the foil and fans the steaming bouquet toward Wendy's bowed head. The bearded porcine chef makes the rounds grinning and chanting, *"Bienvenue, bienvenue."*

Hubert has an unruly flattop and a quick wit. He seems aware of the beauty and absurdity of life, of how much time it takes to roast the exquisite duck he serves, and how little it takes to consume it. At the end of the long rapturous meal, he sends us back to the Montalembert in the restaurant's private car. "Only for you," he says.

"Do you think we could get a jar of that soup to take away?" Sarah asks.

Rue de l'Université after dinner with Brad and Wade. The dark narrow street in the 6th is quiet and moody, the antique shops thoughtfully lit for restless nocturnals.

"Check this out," Wade says. Three startingly white stuffed rabbits are mounted one on top of the other.

"*L'amour du lapin,*" I say. "*L'amour éternel.*"

"Eternal something," Brad says.

"Birds do it, bees do it, even stuffed bunnies do it," Wendy sings.

I can't really explain to Sarah why I think the still lifes of Jean-Baptiste-Siméon Chardin are some of my favorite paintings. I say something about calmness, solidity, the handling of the paint, celebrating everyday life and transcending it at the same time. It has to do with stillness, the absolute immersion in the real and tangible to a degree that makes the peach, the pewter pitcher, the glass of wine completely present and completely timeless. The paintings by Chardin, made in the 18th century, are still a good answer to the what-is-life-all-about question.

Early evening, mid-January, Saint-Germain-des-Prés. *Les soldes.* The sales. Stores are at the boil. Inside one on rue de Grenelle, Sarah tugs on boots with toes sharp as knives. I wait outside. A woman with two large shopping bags lifts her leashed dog into the air when it yelps at two whippets. She yanks the growling mouse off its feet several times, like a yoyo.

The new campaign to have owners pick up after their dogs, rather than city men in little green trucks, is not working – the sidewalks are still a minefield.

Waiters are aflutter. There is bowing, kissing of the lady's hand, stroking of the gentleman's coat. Twirling before the beautiful young woman. "*Je t'adore, ma chérie.*" A rather grand looking woman, a jeweled heart embroidered on her sweater, delicately spoons up chocolate mousse.

This is our last dinner. Sarah tells us about a prince she met, and a famous actor. Tomorrow she leaves for New York. Released from the gilded cage of the restaurant, Wendy says, "We have to go home. I can't eat another thing." She and Sarah walk arm in arm in the river mist. The streets are quiet and so are we.

Le Voltaire
Le

woman with jeweled
heart brooch
Rest aurant
le Voltaire

2003

Wendy is worried. Regis broke his arm. "He will be back," Thierry says. "He has worked here for eighteen years." It's ritual now to have our first dinner in Paris at Le Voltaire. Pascal passes by with a basket of truffles black as coal. Heads turn, noses twitch. He comes back with a roasted *poussin* for Emily.

"What did you see at the Louvre?" Wendy asks.

"Do you think Raphael is overrated?" David asks.

"Don't ask your old art professor that question," I say.

"What is an odalisque exactly?" Emily asks. David met Emily last summer in New Hampshire. She came to France to celebrate New Year's with us.

"I think it's a concubine in a harem," I say. "Did you see the Ingres?"

"Isn't it just a painting of a naked woman on her side?" Wendy says. "They don't have concubines anymore."

Antoine presses an umbrella on us as we gather at the door. "*Il pleut,*" he says softly and smiles a gnomish smile.

"We'll be all right," Wendy says. "We don't have to go far."

"Please. This way I know you will come back."

A doctor with movie star looks and a baritone voice sticks the handle of a toothbrush in my mouth. My toothbrush. "*Dites ahhhh,*" he says. He takes my blood pressure, presses a stethoscope to my chest. He broods, raising a heavy eyebrow once or twice. "Bronchitis," he pronounces with the voice of God. He scribbles a prescription and tells me to get some rest.

"He sure is handsome," Wendy says, closing the door behind him.

"You'd think he would have a couple of tongue depressors in his leather bag," I say. My cough sounds like an explosion on a battlefield.

"I'm glad he makes house calls, or hotel calls."

"I feel worse than I sound, if that's possible."

"I'll go to the pharmacy."

"Don't go chasing the doctor."

Dinner at Aux Fins Gourmets. Cassoulet and rough Basque wine. We rotate seats during the long meal. David lights a cigar as a giant bottle of Armagnac comes to the table with six *verres*. "Who are your three favorite painters?" Brad asks.

"Titian, Manet, Degas," David says without hesitation

"Giorgione, Watteau, Twombly," I say. "Chardin, Matisse, Morandi. You could come up with a lot of good trios."

"Kind of like double-play combos," David says. "Velázquez to Picasso to Rauschenberg. Tinker to Evers to Chance."

"Three favorite women painters?" Wade asks.

"Much harder," Wendy says. "Berthe Morisot, Sonia Delaunay, Joan Mitchell."

"They don't go by their last names?" Emily asks.

"Not yet," David says. "Unfortunately."

First time we have seen it here. Snow, common to us, exotic to Parisians.

Airports close, cars are stranded on autoroutes. Motorbikes and bicycles leaning outside cafés turn ghostly, trees in squares, skeletal. Windshields are scraped with cardboard or credit card. Kids squeal. Snowmen pop up, snowball fights break out. "How do you say when snow and ice *sont ensemble?*" a taxi driver asks. "Hard to drive."

Velázquez, Goya, and Murillo on one side, Courbet, Manet, and Degas on the other. Speaking of double-play combinations. The theme of the show at Musée d'Orsay is the connection between Spanish and French painting.

At the Grand Palais it's Constable as chosen by Lucian Freud. More than a hundred pieces hang in two long rooms. The palace is never a good venue, but this big show is refreshing, not wearying. Mainly because there are more sketches and drawings and small paintings that one hasn't seen, and fewer of the ponderous Constable tableaux of the horse in stream, before field and church tower.

The smaller, more spontaneous works, especially of skies, have a modern charge. Sky in Constable's hands is like flesh in Freud's. Interesting that Freud, a figurative painter, is so in tune with the landscape master. Both are observers of the first rank. Both know how to move paint around, though to quite different effect. Constable said painting is another word for feeling. For Freud, painting may be another word for thinking.

"Why aren't American cities more attractive? Brad asks. "Why doesn't Minneapolis have more manmade beauty?"

"It should," Wade says. "It's progressive, prosperous, educated."

"It's happy with lakes and parks," Wendy says.

"We saw a model of the Robie House today," I say, "designed by Frank Lloyd Wright. Pretty good example of manmade beauty."

"It's around the corner from where I grew up in Hyde Park," Wendy says. "By the university. I used to walk on the wall in front of the Robie House when I was a girl."

"Didn't your father save the Robie House?"

"Papa literally took the key from the crane with the wrecking ball. He was walking by on his way to the law school."

"Wow," Wade says. "It was that close. Usually we tear down the beautiful and replace it with the ugly."

"Wright's family was burned and axed by one of his

servants," Brad says. "The cook, I think."

"Nice dinner topic," Wade says.

"Didn't like his architecture?" David says.

"*Excusez-moi,*" the portly maître d' says as he squeezes through a narrow door by our table and disappears into the cellar. He returns with several bottles of wine. "How is your dinner?" he asks.

"Very good," I say. "Compliments to the chef."

"Always compliment the chef," David says.

Victor Hugo is full of surprises. He lived in the mid-1800s on the second floor of a corner mansion overlooking Place des Vosges. The Hugo residence, now a museum, is dark and romantic like his writing. Rich fabrics cover the walls, the furniture is medieval. The remarkable Chinese room is filled floor to ceiling with painted carved wood, porcelain, and figurines. Hugo wrote here, of course, including a good deal of *Les Misérables.* But who knew he decorated the place himself.

Hugo was also a gifted draftsman. A group of his drawings are on display the cold day we visit the museum. The mysterious, surreal works done with brush and pen in sepia and black ink are quite unexpected.

His drawings (he made thousands) include grotesque caricatures, landscapes, and pure abstractions of inkblots, floating stains, and random fluid brushstrokes. These last are the best. Organic and unfinished, they have a spooky, dreamlike quality. He sometimes splashed a sheet with coffee and often made patterns with lace. Flaubert said, "Hugo isn't a thinker; he's a naturalist. He is waist-deep in nature. He has got the sap of trees in his blood."

Though he died in Paris, Hugo lived for some time as an exile on Guernsey in an extravagant house by the sea that his son called "a poem in several rooms." Writer, artist, maker of interiors, Hugo was also politically active, railing against the injustices of the day. When Napoleon III seized power, Hugo left the country. "What is France?" he said. "An idea. Paris? I have no need of Paris. Paris is the rue de Rivoli, and I have always loathed the rue de Rivoli."

The waiter slides nimbly past our table. "*J'arrive, j'arrive,*" he says. Why is Café de Flore busy when other cafés are not? It's not just because of its history. Wendy chats with the woman next to us, a musician from New York. Two Japanese women study the menu as if it's the Magna Carta. A man, with Cocteau nose and hair, frowns at *Le Monde* through a cumulus of cigarette smoke.

The café serves croque monsieurs and croque madames to people from all over the world and to a lot of Parisians. It's expensive but well-run, chic but democratic. A waiter hands the Japanese women a menu in Japanese as he strides toward the kitchen. "*Un espress,*" he yells. Catherine Deneuve walks in. The man with the Cocteau nose smiles and stands up.

St.
Place Sulpice

The sky is a pale, ironic blue. It is *très froid*. We walk anyway to the Place Saint-Sulpice. The lions in front of the church are still. No water flows in the Visconti fountain today. In the Jardin du Luxembourg a man clears the tennis courts of snow with a leaf blower. Young chestnut and linden trees have been planted to replace those destroyed in *la tempête* of '99.

Who is bundled more against the cold: women on the streets of Saint-Germain-des-Prés or their dogs? Roles are reversed. *Les dames* wear fur, *les chiens* wear clothes. The cashier in one posh Italian store wears her full-length coat inside. We stop in Il Bisonte, the Italian leather goods store. "I could go in here for the smell alone," I say. It smells of leather the way Poilâne across the street smells of bread. Like many, we were sad to hear that Lionel Poilâne, owner of the venerable family bakery, died recently in a plane crash.

"Smells take your mind off the cold," Wendy says.

"Even the smell of fish," I say as we pass the fishmonger on rue du Bac that opens on to the street. Across Boulevard Saint-Germain, we go into Au Nom de la Rose, where Wendy buries her face in the buckets of flowers. "Smell," she says.

"Ah," I say, "Roses make me feel immortal."

"Which color do you prefer? Immortal white or immortal red?"

Ladurée has just opened a shop on rue Jacob, under the apartment of James Ivory and Ismail Merchant. A pale pistachio green on the outside, it's pretty enough to be a setting in one of their movies. On the walls of the tearoom are murals of lush banana palms and parrots. "I feel like I'm on an island in the Caribbean," Wendy says.

"Does it make you feel warmer?"

"This will." She pours hot chocolate from the pot into our cups.

"Smells like heaven but it's hot as hell."

Lightly fried baby squid, a grilled sea bass with eggplant, an excellent Meursault, tart lemon tart, strong espresso. It is all presented proudly by a corpulent man wearing a blue Breton jacket who is obsessive about fish. The perfect meal?

We laugh and reminisce about the old days, in the early 70s (before kids), when we stopped at a dozen restaurants in the 5th or 6th, perused menus, and glanced through windows until we finally chose one. The days before we all turned into demanding connoisseurs of the table, daring not for a second to go into a place that isn't vetted and blessed by some trusted authority or friend.

Tonight's restaurant, rightly blessed for its seafood, is across the street from the Montalembert, a brief walk in the frigid night. Yes, a perfect meal, the stars are aligned. Another night they are not aligned. After a delightful meal in a new restaurant on the Quai de Bourbon, where the scallops with risotto is served in a Japanese bowl by a lanky Dutchman, our talk about buying or renting an apartment in Paris ends in anger. "You're a bully," Wendy says.

We trudge back along a quiet Boulevard Saint-Germain twenty paces apart. It's a long walk. "Hey," I say, running to catch up, "didn't we eat in that place thirty years ago?"

A beautiful painting on a wall or ceiling seems purer than a beautiful painting on wood or canvas. A fresco, unlike a painting, can't be bought or sold. It is meant to be appreciated, not to appreciate, to enrich the soul, not the bank account. Unless of course you have the fortune, both good and large, bestowed upon the 19th-century art lovers Édouard André and Nélie Jacquemart.

They built a mansion, near what is now Parc Monceau, for their many-splendored collection, the glory of which is a Tiepolo fresco over twenty feet wide, taken from a wall in the Villa Contarini in Venice. Mounted on canvas, it hangs at the top of the mansion's grand staircase. To take in fully the airy panorama of a Venetian doge welcoming a French king, you have to stand on a narrow landing on the other side of a wide atrium. The Jacquemart-André is the only French museum with a Tiepolo fresco.

Actually it has several. The ceiling fresco in the museum restaurant, also from the Venetian villa, shows putti in a wispy sky announcing the arrival of the king. Around the edges of the fresco, propped against the painted balustrade, are dressed-up Venetians looking down, not on the king, but on you and your *tarte aux framboises.*

Edouard and Nélie were especially fond of Italian works. In the downstairs Florentine Gallery, Uccello's dragon, with its perfectly thrice-coiled pig's tail, fanned wing of black dots, and red throat run through by Saint George's lance, is both fierce and childlike. Though grand, the house has a personal feel as the library, smoking room, and bedrooms are still intact. The interior winter garden provides for the visitor as surely as it must have for the avid collectors respite from dragons, madonnas, and tapestries.

Alain Passard welcomes tonight's guests to his small modern restaurant on rue de Varenne. He is in jeans and tennis shoes, his guests are in ties and jewels. The rounded, pear wood walls suggest the shape of a woman.

Before Wendy are tiny martini glasses of caviar and cream. In front of me is a plate of sliced celery root and chestnuts in a coriander sauce. "I'll return with the truffle," the waiter says.

"Are exotic foods like truffles and caviar acquired tastes?"

"I liked caviar the first time I had it as a child. Don't talk, eat."

"Is it because they are expensive or hard to come by?"

"It's because they're delicious."

The chef sits down with friends. Moments later a small mountain of salt on a platter is delivered to their table. Passard takes a knife and cracks through the dense white chrystals to the gold inside. We watch fascinated. "Potatoes," I say amazed.

"Doesn't get more exotic than that," Wendy says.

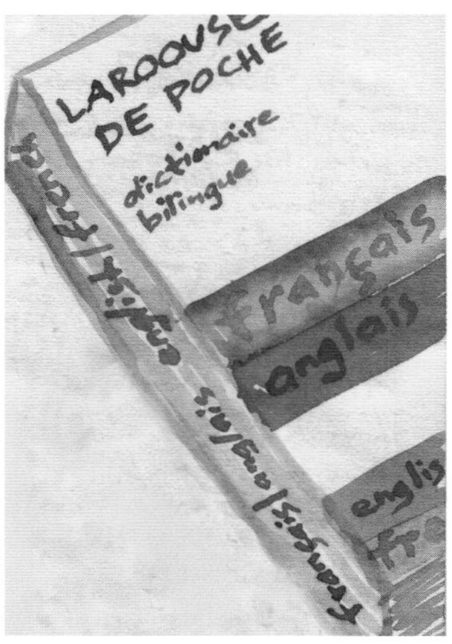

Rows of lime trees, leafless, tops cropped, line the courtyard of the Palais Royal like members of a winter guard. Even the trees look cold. A kitchen crew, impervious in white short sleeves, smokes under an arcade. Can't stand the heat, but how can they stand the icy air? Wrapped in blankets almost to invisibility a woman sits in a chair, face upturned to the weak sun. A skinny dog looks up the leash at his master talking on a cell phone. Shivering, the dog is unhappy that nature and girlfriend have called at the same time.

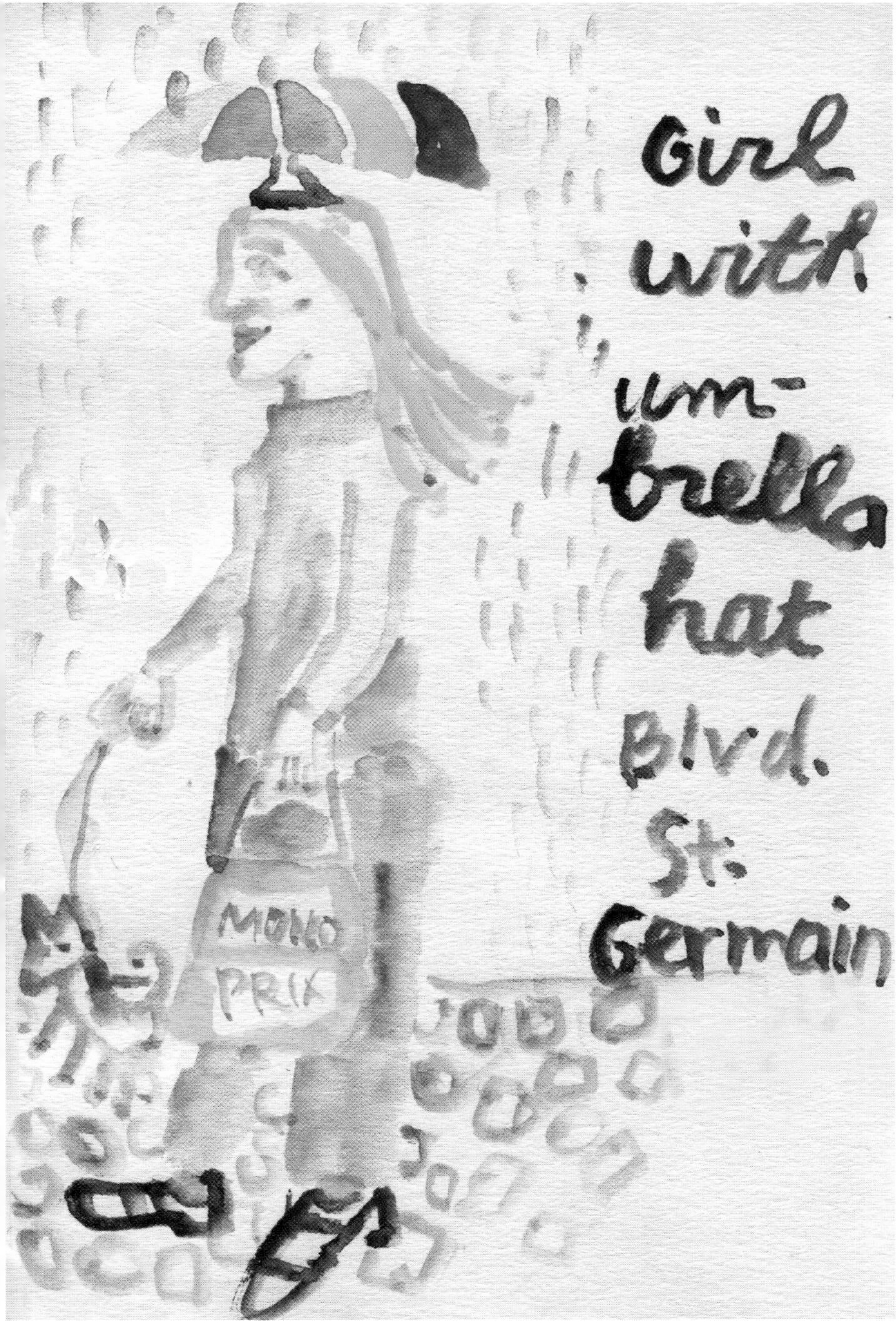

Girl with um-brella hat Blvd. St. Germain

Rows of books lining shelves of a library emanate warmth. Maybe that's why the reading room in the Richelieu branch of the Bibliothèque Nationale is full. Mile high stacks of books rise behind arched columns to circular windows that form a ring around a giant oval skylight that echoes the oval room below. It's a stunning space designed in the mid 19th century by the major, but little known, French architect Henri Labrouste.

In the Mansart Gallery is an exhibition called "The First Thirty Books." Elaborately bound and studded with jewels, the books are part of the immense library assembled by librarian Gabriel Naudé for Cardinal Mazarin, chief minister of France in the 17th century. Housed here in Mazarin's palace until his death, when they were moved to the Institut de France across the river, the collection formed the basis of the first public library in France.

On view, and most important perhaps of all the world's books, is the Gutenberg Bible, the first book published with movable type, the progenitor of modern books, and arguably modern thought. One of forty-nine copies still in existence, this Gutenberg is called the Mazarin. Gutenberg printed the Bible in the 1450s. It was discovered in the cardinal's library in 1740 long after he was dead and it lies now in front of us in 2003.

Modigliani wanted to be a sculptor. This may explain the ovoid forms he uses to depict people in his paintings, a great number of which are at the Musée du Luxembourg. Modigliani's work seems formulaic, all caricature and hollow eyes, painted in a hurry. Yesterday it was "The First Thirty Books," today "The Fastest Fifty Paintings."

Perhaps Modigliani is a young person's artist. Perhaps

he knew he had to paint quickly because he didn't have a lot of time. His life was tragic. Born into a bourgeois Italian family, he became in Paris the prototypical bohemian artist. He was charismatic, handsome, a lover of women. He drank and took drugs in part because he wanted to hide from others the tuberculosis that was killing him. Jeanne, his beautiful, common-law wife, nine months pregnant, jumped from a window the day after he died. He was thirty-six, she was twenty.

Modigliani sold few paintings in his life.

The Seine today is a churning, murky tea. A barge named *Minnesota* passes under a bridge carrying a pile of coal, or maybe it's truffles.

Over the bridge, in fading light, comes a river of rollerbladers. There are well over a hundred. Policemen on horseback stop traffic and pedestrians to let them stream by. A few days ago near the Tuileries we saw several policemen clicking along on rollerblades. I wonder if a blader cop ever catches a bad guy?

"*Votre dernière soirée à Paris?*" Antoine asks.

"Yes, sadly," Wendy says.

Two French couples next to us are talking about *Bowling for Columbine* and Charlton Heston. A small bulldog lies at the feet of a man eating with his mother. The man is wearing horn-rimmed glasses and socks that match the green of his pocket handkerchief.

"*Vous avez une belle signature,*" Antoine says as I sign the bill.

Thierry takes Wendy's hand in his, then gives her a hug. "*À la prochaine,*" he says. "*Bon retour.*"

On the corner of rue de Beaune we stop to admire the little Italian painting in the window. We have swooned over it almost every day since we arrived three weeks ago.

Dawn, the sky is still dark. The streets are empty, the city asleep. The Eiffel Tower is a luminous steeple, a column of embers. The car to the airport crosses the river.

2004

In our room orchids, mandarin oranges, champagne. A Bernese mountain dog is in the lobby. "Maybe we'll bring Bella over one year."

"Two seats for us," Wendy says. "Two seats for her."

"I heard Swiss Air gives discounts for Berners."

"*Bonne année,*" says Renaud, the Montalembert concierge. "Welcome back to Paris."

"*Merci,* Renaud. How are you?"

"*Bonjour, Monsieur et Madame Coggins.*" Fabien, in smart double-breasted coat, tips his cap and pushes open the door.

"*Bonjour, Fabien.* You look handsome as always."

We have lunch in the Marais with Dominique Serrand and Sarah Agnew. Dominique is an old friend. Born in Paris into a distinguished family, he has lived in the U.S. for over thirty years and is director of a theater company. He and Sarah, an American actress, were married five years ago at the Serrand family château. They are in Paris for his father's eightieth birthday. "We've seen some good theater," Sarah says. "Mnouchkine's *Le Dernier Caravansérail* at La Cartoucherie."

"And *Ta main dans la mienne,*" Dominique says. "Peter Brook directed. Michel Piccoli plays Chekhov. It's based on letters between Chekhov and his wife."

"I take your hand in mine," Sarah says. "It's what Chekhov wrote to Olga, his wife."

Dominique takes us to the Hôtel de Beauvais on rue François-Miron. We stand in the cobbled courtyard and take in the mansion's Baroque, semi-circular façade. "This courtyard was once used as a theater," Dominique says.

The house was built in the 17th century for a Monsieur de Beauvais after his wife took to bed the virginal Louis XIV, with the complicity of the teenager's mother, Anne of Austria. Monsieur's wife was Anne's handmaiden, and the palace, a reward for her role as instructress. One assumes for such compensation Monsieur de Beauvais gave his blessing to the event.

zebra
Deyrolle

A century later another boy became part of the history of the Hôtel de Beauvais. Mozart, all of seven, stayed in the palace when he came to Paris on tour with his father and sister. He too had to perform, but in concert, not *au lit.*

Much loved Deyrolle has been "made over" by its new owner, a prince. The first floor has become a swishy garden shop. The time-layered atmosphere on the taxidermy floor is gone. At the top of the stairs is a familiar crowd of savannah creatures – giraffe, antelope, zebra, ostrich – but they now stand around a long table, set for dinner in a bright green room. They look embarrassed.

The fragile 18th-century rooms are still rife with butterflies and beetles, shells and rocks, but it's been spiffed up. Deyrolle feels less like an eccentric private collection that hasn't been touched in decades, and more like a store. Commerce trumps personality.

David arrives from Zurich, chipper and dapper in coat and tie. We have dinner at L'Atelier, Joël Robuchon's new restaurant. We sit at a counter, as does everyone, in slick dark rooms. It's a pretty fancy diner.

"Still no word from Sarah?" I ask. "Where exactly is she in Ireland?"

"Somewhere in the countryside," Wendy says.

"I'm not sure Sarah knows exactly what kippers are," David says.

"I'm not sure I do," I say. "I'm not sure I want to."

Before us, a group of young chefs clad in black prepare with surgical finesse a great number of refined dishes having nothing to do with kippers. Steamed sea bass, caramelized quail, and chartreuse soufflés are served on square plates by bright young staff, also dressed in black.

David
at the Louvre

"Feels a little like Rembrandt's *Anatomy Lesson,*" David says, "watching these cooks go to town."

"Kitchen as theater," I say.

"Isn't that Joël Robuchon?" Wendy asks.

"That's the head waiter."

I love Vuillard, but not enough of his small intimate interiors are at the hot, crowded Grand Palais. The artist lived with his mother, a corset maker, until he was sixty. He was surrounded by women, by flowered dresses and patterned walls, by quiet domesticity. His best work was done before 1900, though he worked prolifically after that, and got out from under his mother's skirts into grander Parisian society. He died in 1940.

The early work captures the life immediately at hand: family and friends doing mundane things like having breakfast, sewing, and reading. Private scenes in oil paint built up in dense, juxtaposed patterns on cardboard. The Vuillard apartment door opens, as if by mistake, and you peer into a cloistered world. You want to apologize and move on, but the scene is magnetic and luminous and not without tension. Vuillard lets us look, perhaps against his will.

David leads us on a pilgrimage to the 2nd, where A.J. Liebling lived as an apprentice gourmand in the 1920s. He lived in the Hôtel Louvois on Square Louvois. A fountain in the square streams water over four stone maidens.

Liebling's *Between Meals* is one of David's favorite books. One episode involves Liebling dining out with his family visiting from America. "I brought my family here because I was told this is the most illustrious house of Paris," Liebling tells the restaurant owner. "My father is the richest man in Baltimore. We desire to knock the bell." Whenever David studies the menu at a good restaurant, he says, "I desire to knock the bell."

Some of the best lines Liebling ever wrote are on the first page of *Between Meals.*

> *In the light of what Proust wrote with so mild a stimulus, it is the world's loss that he did not have a heartier appetite. On a dozen Gardiner Island oysters, a bowl of clam chowder, a peck of steamers, some bay scallops, three sautéed soft-shelled crabs, a few ears of fresh picked corn, a thin swordfish steak of generous area, a pair of lobsters, and a Long Island duck, he might have written a masterpiece.*

On Boulevard Saint-Germain an older couple and their long-haired dachshund clamber out of a Camaro. The dog, whose leash is links of plastic sausages, is the most stylish of the three.

In Café l'Éspérance on the corner of rue de l'Université and rue du Bac a woman snaps the ends off *les haricots verts* and puts the long thin beans into a big bowl on the table. *"Bonjour,"* she trills as we enter. *"Ça va bien?"* The snapping and trilling continue throughout breakfast.

The French write in little notebooks in museums. Dense cramped handwriting. Look with great seriousness at a painting, then write meticulously.

A taxi driver from Tunisia chats with us. He can't quite get over the fact that we Americans speak some French. He flashes a big smile when he looks into his rearview mirror. In another taxi there is no talking. "Così fan tutte" is on the radio.

Cafe de
la
Paix
AU
BON
MARCHÉ

Looking up from rue de Rennes one budding January night I am surprised to see a round sallow moon. Grayed by city lights, it shines faintly down on Parisians as they head home or to cafés, done with the day's work and with "le shopping" at the sales. Briefcases and bags swing along the *rues*. It shines on me. I have no bag, no place to go. Maybe that's why I looked up.

On rue de l'Université a fashionable woman cries out *"Gizmo! Gizmo!"* She looks around frantically. *"Où est mon chien? Gizmo! Gizmo!"* We turn on rue de Beaune. A lap dog dragging its leash, looking for its lap, runs by.

The portrait of Le comte Robert de Montesquiou by Giovanni Boldini hangs in the Musée d'Orsay. I always stop to look at it. The count was, in his turn-of-the-twentieth-century Baudelairian era, a pompous aristocrat and an aesthete, a handsome dandy purveying extravagant dress, conversation, and manner. With the perfect trifecta of arched dark eyebrows, pomaded villain's moustache, and aquiline nose, how could he not be a "symbolic poet." White gloves and cane, too. Boldini does not paint him smiling – he had black teeth.

Montesquiou was reportedly a model for Proust's Baron de Charlus and Huysmans' des Esseintes in *À rebours.* Among his possessions in "The Pavilion of the Muses," his home on rue Franklin, were the bullet that killed Pushkin, the slippers of a woman who loved Byron, and Napoleon's bedpan. He was quoted as saying, "One should always listen to von Weber in mauve," and was said to have slept with only one person, Sarah Bernhardt. He threw up afterwards. Can any of this be true?

The pedestrian streets near the beautiful Saint-Eustache church, in the old Les Halles quarter, crackle with life. Humanity in all sizes and colors swarms the cobblestones, the shops, and cafés. Molière, whose funeral was at Saint-Eustache, would be inspired by this *comédie de la rue,* by the faces and follies of 21st-century Paris.

"Feel like a kebab?" I say pointing to Restaurant Zam Zam.

The faded Michelin from Wendy's first trip to Paris with her family in 1960 lists the names of a few restaurants around the huge market, which was going strong in those days. Traditional French places like Au Chien Qui Fume and Au Pied de Cochon are still open. The market fed Paris for hundreds of years until it was destroyed in the 1970s. Over twenty acres in size, the belly of Paris, as Zola christened it (*Le Ventre de Paris* was one of his novels), was as remarkable for its architecture as for its food stalls. The pavilions, built in the mid 19th century of arched metal frames and glass roofs, were light and airy and soared like the new train stations of the day.

"Do you remember going to Les Halles?" I ask Wendy.

"Yes, it was overwhelming."

"I wish I had seen it. Did you eat pigs' feet?"

"My mother ate *tête de veau* once."

"I could eat pigs' feet given enough wine."

"You or the pigs' feet?"

Galerie Véro-Dodat was named after two butchers. In 1826, Monsieur Véro and Monsieur Dodat opened charcuteries in the arcade, a new commercial and structural wonder. We pass under the small balcony on rue Jean-Jacques Rousseau and enter the glass-roofed passage. Shops and cafés with wooden fronts and white ball lamps line the black and white tiled hall. It's a place of refuge – elegant, nostalgic, quiet.

One of 150 built in the 19th century, the arcade gave Parisians a sheltered place to shop and take their leisure away from weather and streets overrun with carriages and sewage. They were highly popular until Le Bon Marché came along. Only about twenty remain. Some have been restored. Galerie Véro-Dodat was the first mall. It gave birth to Southdale, America's first indoor shopping mall.

Walter Benjamin thought the *passages couvert* expressed something essential about 19th-century Paris. He felt the blend of architecture, business, and social life held the secret to modern life. He spent years compiling thousands of quotes and fragments of writing from 19th-century figures like Baudelaire, but also from Proust, Breton, and later writers. Combined with his own commentary, this material, epic in scale and unfinished at his death in 1940, was published in the 1980s.

The Arcades Project, at a thousand pages, is something to dip in and out of, which is perhaps what Benjamin intended. It's a kaleidoscopic way of looking at the past, not by focusing on great people and events, but on less visible aspects of collective daily life, on bits and pieces that when put together offer a different, perhaps truer picture. Some think Benjamin's postmodern montage extraordinary, others think it superficial hodgepodge.

On the Place du Palais-Royal, athletic *jeunes hommes* on rollerblades zig and zag, click and clack around each other. They kick and chase a ball. Pedestrians give them wide berth. Soccer Zam Zam.

In the Louvre des Antiquaires, an immense ceramic vase outside one shop crashes to the floor. People stop and stare as if at a car accident. No one seems to know how it happened.

Sarah arrives after a week with Colm and his friends in County Cork and on the island of Cape Clear. She has us laughing from the get go as we settle in at Le Voltaire.

"There's no heat in Ireland. What do you expect from fires made of peat? I've been wet and cold all week."

"It is January," David says. "What did you do?"

"Hiked in Wellies, slept in a bunk bed, ate porridge, drank Guinness."

"Kippers?"

"Had kippers. Once. Eiffa plucked sheep's wool from brambles for weaving. They're all hippies. Sweet lovely people. I had a great time, but I'm glad to be in Paris."

"How about a glass of champagne?" I ask.

"How about some shopping? My wardrobe is a little depleted."

"The sales are on," Wendy says.

"How fortunate."

"Do you want to share a *côte de boeuf?*" David asks his sister.

"Sure, which side?"

David and Sarah (in glittering new heels) vanish into the Paris night. Wendy and I walk along rue de Beaune. The air is cool and fresh. Walking after dinner is all the nightlife we need. Footsteps echo in the quiet streets. Old chairs and vases and paintings from the sea of unknown rooms fill the antique shops like shells on a beach. A woman on a bicycle passes like a deer in the forest.

Fragonard's drawings grace a dark intimate room in the Louvre. Medallion self-portraits in black chalk and tender portraits of his son and daughter. Fragonard was born in Grasse, the city of roses and perfumes. His father was a glove maker. Wendy and I visited his house in Grasse one fall, years ago. It had been raining, I remember, and a few flowers clung to the bushes. There was a faint smell of dead leaves and earth, but not of flowers.

David and I recently saw Fragonard's *The Progress of Love* panels at the Frick. We had gone there in the midst of a Manhattan blizzard. The panels were originally painted for a country pavilion built for the Comtesse du Barry, a mistress of Louis XV, in the late 18th century. Fragonard, acclaimed and prolific in the Rococo world before the revolution, died a forgotten man. I won't forget looking out at the Frick gardens covered in deep snow and I won't forget Fragonard's young lovers in bright gardens.

We venture into Maille, the famous mustard shop on Place de la Madeleine. People line up to get empty ceramic jars filled with the tangy mustard. A jolly woman pulls a spigot on a giant vat and *la moutarde* streams out. Regular customers have their own Maille pots. Wendy finds a new black jar and gets in line.

"Come back when it is empty," the woman tells her.

Wendy
Palais Royal

"We live in America."

"Pas de problème. Bring your pot when you come back to Paris."

David flies home to New York, leaving us in Paris rain. We jump puddles across the Pont de Sully, stopping to take in the view across the river of the east and south sides of Notre-Dame. "I like this view of the church better than the front view," Sarah says.

"You can see the rose window," Wendy says. "And the buttresses flying."

We linger in the park behind the church where Sarah and David played when we first came to Paris with them in 1982. Linger again in front of Hôtel de Lutèce on rue Saint-Louis en l'Île where we stayed on that first trip.

"Yes, I know, Dad, I was three and David was six," Sarah says.

"And we went to the . . . ," I say.

"To Berthillon for ice cream across the street."

"What flavors?"

"I don't remember. Do you?"

"No."

"That's why I don't remember."

The Île Saint-Louis, a village in the middle of the river, is one of the most beautiful spots in Paris despite having become a major tourist flyway. I remember in the early 70s when Wendy and I first came to Paris and the street felt local and undiscovered. I was so taken with it I wanted to live there.

We cross over to the right bank on Pont Louis-Philippe, stopping again to look at the spires of Notre-Dame behind the Quai de Bourbon. Minutes after entering the Marais, Wendy and Sarah disappear into a shop. It's the cosmo shift. Church to store, buttress to dress, sacred to secular. Benjamin would have something to say about this.

"*On est ce que l'on garde!*" Nothing could be more true of the man who once uttered these words. Picasso tells you what kind of man he was as much by what he saved as by what he painted. A lot of what he saved (and he saved everything) is on view at the Musée Picasso. The museum is in the former Hôtel Salé, a mansion in the Marais built in the 17th century by a man who collected taxes on salt. The grandeur of the house seems fitting for a museum devoted to Picasso and so does the old name. *Salé* means salty.

There are thousands of notebooks, letters, tickets, address books, sketches. Mind-boggling, even to one who shares the same obsession. He knew everybody, or everybody knew him. Batches of letters tied up in string, letters back-lit spread across walls, stacks of archival boxes surrounding items from Dalí, Braque, Matisse, and countless others.

"Lots of stuff," Sarah says.

"See what happens when you save everything," Wendy says.

"They put it in a museum," I say.

"Only if you are Picasso. And you have your own museum."

"I might one day. *Musée de Stuff.*"

The Musée Baccarat is in another grand old house – the former *hôtel particulier* of Marie-Laure de Noailles, lavish arts patron and great-great-great granddaughter of the Marquis de Sade. The museum is on Place des États-Unis in the 16th. Designed by Philippe Starck, it opened in 2003. What would Jean-Michel Frank, who decorated the house in the 1920s, make of the immense crystal chandelier in a tank of water? Other Starckian touches: video faces in wall sconces, carpets lined with tiny lights, a chair for a giant, and a half-log sofa with a metal rod back. That's before you get to the galleries.

The first salon is all vanitas: nothing but floor to ceiling mirrors, gilt, and chandeliers hanging like bats. A tent in one room encloses vitrines of old Baccarat. A darkened room shows antique vases, glasses, and pitchers to dramatic effect. Another has a one-ton chandelier made for a Russian czar. In the boutique, on a table fifty feet long, Wendy finds wine glasses made for today's bourgeoisie.

"I've spent a lot of time in England," Jacques says, accounting for his quick fluent English. He runs to the café next door for espressos. "I love New York and London. Paris is boring, don't you think? Do you take sugar?" The high-spirited antique dealer tosses off dates and periods of furniture as if names of family members. The mix of objects in his shop, Galerie Hervouet on rue de l'Université, is odd and alluring. We leave with a 19th-century tea box and the feeling we have made a friend.

The philosopher Bernard-Henri Lévy and his actress wife sit at a table by the front window. They seem too glamorous for the laid back Aux Fins Gourmets. He, with black jacket, unbuttoned white shirt, and troubadour hair, seems too glamorous for a philosopher. Aux Fins Gourmets is more patched cardigan and receding hairline. Certainly plenty of self-styled bistro philosophers have eaten here. We are at a table in the back.

"How long have you been in New York?" Brad asks Sarah.

"Two years. I like Paris more," she says. "It's gentler."

"New York is masculine," Wendy says. "Paris is feminine."

More Margaux, more talk about living here. I draw on the paper tablecloth. The ashtray fills up. To Café de Flore for nightcaps. More people watching and gossiping and laughing and pretending to pretend to be Parisian. A waiter spills champagne on a woman's laptop open on the table. "Did he do that on purpose?" Brad asks.

While Wendy and Sarah go to the Louvre to see the African collection, I promenade. Long before Catherine de' Medici turned the Tuileries into a private park, it was a quarry where men dug up clay to make tiles for roofs. Tile in French is *tuile;* the workshops were called *tuileries.*

Once royals and courtiers in satin shoes strolled arm in arm through the gardens. Now citizens of the world cling to the arms of green chairs, prop up tennis shoes and muddy boots, and watch ducks paddle about and children push sailboats. I walk among the ponds and sculpture then settle into a chair myself. The sun warms, the crowd amuses.

Sunday, Jardin du Luxembourg, after a night of rain and a morning of church bells. Two girls with pastel coats tiptoe on the grass. Mother and father gather them up. Scouts in berets and long shorts walk in a kind of group circle, gesturing and joking. Runners circle the park like moons around a planet. We head for the apiary, past the sign warning of bees. Gold leaf bees painted on the gatepost are scratched and faded. Behind the fence, hives inside wooden houses with copper roofs are dormant.

"I saw a man pushing a bass fiddle down the street yesterday," I say.

"I played bass fiddle in grade school," Wendy says. "Mr. Mason was my teacher. He was really old. Thank god, he was deaf. I couldn't read music."

"I don't know which is harder to imagine. You as a little girl playing bass fiddle or a deaf music teacher."

Runners. "You know, *Maman,* I've never seen you run," Sarah says. Wendy gamely pulls up her long coat and high steps a few yards down the wet path. Across from the gardens, on Square Francis-Poulenc, we look in a shop window filled with old children's games. Children are everywhere in Paris, bright and precocious.

In Ladurée a polite young woman slips her hand into a surgeon's glove, takes colorful *macarons* from the rows on display, and nestles them one by one into a tissue-lined black and white box with a bulldog on it. "So *Franche,*" Wendy says.

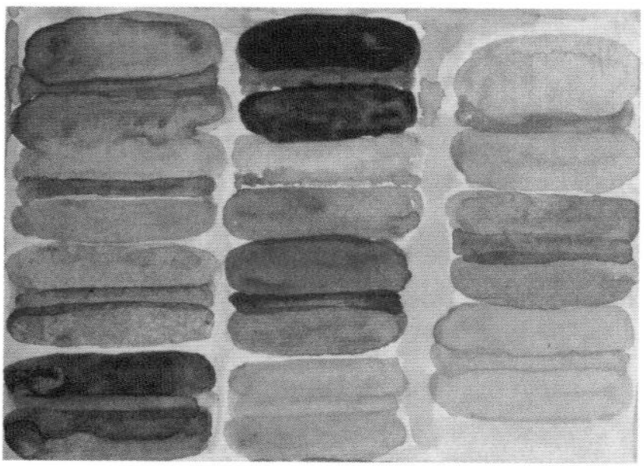

We order cheese and wine to the room and watch *The Sheltering Sky*. "I like not having to go out every night," Sarah says.

"We can go to the café for coffee later," Wendy says.

At the end of the film Paul Bowles appears as narrator and speaks these famous words: "Because we don't know when we will die, we get to think of life as an inexhaustible well. Yet everything happens a certain number of times, and a very small number, really.... How many more times will you watch the full moon rise? Perhaps twenty. And yet it all seems limitless."

"How many more times will we walk the streets of Paris?" I ask dramatically.

"A few hundred, *plus ou moins,*" Sarah says.

Sophie Calle is having a moment. The Centre Pompidou has mounted a retrospective of her highly conceptual work. The *chef d'oeuvre* is a winding line of photographs. First are photos of her in Japan before her lover breaks off their relationship. This part is called "Avant la Douleur." "Après la Douleur" are photos of the room in Delhi where she learned of the breakup.

The photos are interspersed with images and words related to pain and suffering. Other works are about blindness, loss, and tragedy. It's a fascinating show, though the idea of compassion seems more the point than compassion itself. There may be more to read than to look at.

At lunch in the museum restaurant overlooking the city, the waiter peers down at our table through a mass of unruly hair. He seems distracted and sad as he pours the wine. Perhaps he has just broken up with the statuesque African woman in a flowing dress who hands us our coats and bids us a *très bon après-midi.*

At the Puces de Vanves flea market, Wendy acquires old dibbles. Sarah, negotiating like a pro, fills bags with African jewelry. I buy a beaten-up painting from a kind woman who is about to put it back in her van.

"*Vous êtes dérangé,*" one dealer says to a man standing in front of his table of curios.

"*Peut-être,*" the man replies and makes a counter offer which the dealer readily accepts.

Dinner at Pierre Gagnaire. A meal to end all meals – well, to end our stay in Paris. We are literally unbuttoning and unbuckling at the end. Each course comes with four or five variations on a theme, like "*Orientale,*" and with liberal use of exotic foods and spices. Chef as jazz virtuouso, or perverse genius.

Pigeon is served with sweet plum and sumac and a tower of multicolored vegetables in a saffron sauce. Sarah's turbot with leeks and asparagus has a sauce that drains into a bowl of minced salsify, spooned up after the plate is removed.

At Charles de Gaulle, we bid farewell to Sarah.

"You're the top, you're a Voltaire dinner," I sing to her. "You're the top, you're Paris in winter. You're crème brûlée, you're Ladurée. You're Claude Monet."

"*Bon voyage,*" Wendy says.

"*Bon régime,*" Sarah says and laughs.

2005

Sarah is a resident of Paris. She's going to study fashion at Parsons School of Art and Design. We help install her in a tiny apartment on rue Dupin in the 6th. It has thick wooden beams, a closet-sized kitchen, and a short supply of hot water. The Boulevard Raspail market is around the corner and the restaurant L'Epi Dupin is on the ground floor, a mere five floors down. Sarah throws saris and scarves over the rustic furniture, puts pictures, books, and flowers around.

"Not much of a view," I say standing on the little balcony looking across the street at a vast Soviet-style apartment building.

"But there's lots of light," Sarah says. "And Le Bon Marché is half a block away."

She celebrates New Year's with Sébastien, a Frenchman she met last year in London. "Did you have fun?" I ask.

"I did. I think he did."

"Will you see him again?"

"Maybe."

Sarah likes to go out. She collects Brad and his German friend Alexander and they go dancing at clubs straight and gay. "Brad and I watched *West Side Story* in my apartment," Sarah says. "It was six when I went to bed."

"How was New Year's?" Wendy asks.

"I plucked a duck," David says. "At Laura's farm in Wales."

"My brothers went hunting," Laura says. "We had duck for New Year's dinner."

"What about the buckshot?" Sarah says.

It's lunchtime. We are at Le Grand Véfour. Wendy, Sarah, and Laura sit on the banquette across from David and me. "Here's to the ladies," I say, lifting a glass of champagne. "Beautiful, vibrant, and…."

"Hungry," Sarah says.

"Who's going to have the sea urchins?"

"I'm having *lièvre à la royale,*" David announces.

"What's that?" Sarah says.

"Hare in a dark sauce. It was made for a king who had no teeth. It cooks for days so it falls off the bone. You don't have to chew it. They throw in some foie gras, too."

"You made that up," Laura says.

"Do they pluck the hare?" Sarah says.

"I think they call it skinning."

David met Laura when they were both studying in Paris ten years ago. They met again in London last summer when he was working for the magazine *Modern Painters.* Laura is lovely with dark hair and dark eyes and a smart English accent. All London turned out for the opening of her new gallery last fall.

"I'll have the sea urchins, too," David says. "I desire to knock the bell."

After a postprandial waltz through the Palais Royal and by the shops on rue Saint-Honoré, we circle the Place Vendôme. Pleasure and beauty commingle in the long afternoon. Laughing at an elegant table, strolling arm in arm in a winter garden, enjoying the embrace of an ancient city. It's Paris distilled: concentrated, ethereal, civilized.

The five-year renovation of the Apollo Gallery in the Louvre is complete. The fresh gilt on the heavily ornamented walls and forty-five-foot high ceiling would please Apollo. The vast hall runs over with paintings, sculpture, and tapestries, much of which harks back to 17th-century painter Charles Le Brun and his design for the hall.

It was left half-finished when the Sun King turned his radiant beam on Versailles, though most of Le Brun's paintings remain. A renovation in the 19th century brought in Delacroix's *Apollo Slays Python* to add more grandeur.

The eyes tire, the neck aches. Closer at hand and also dazzling is an assortment of royal jewels, including the Regent diamond, one of the largest and purest in the world, and one of the most legendary. It has been everywhere, from India, where it was found by a slave, to England, where a jeweler named Harris cut the rough stone from over four hundred to one hundred forty carats, to France in 1717 when Philippe II purchased it. It was stolen during the revolution and turned up in a Paris attic. Louis XV wore it in his coronation crown, Marie Antoinette on her hat, Napoleon on his sword. It finally came to rest in a diadem made for Empress Eugénie on display in the Apollo Gallery.

One morning at Café l'Espérance where we often go for breakfast or lunch, we bump into Jacques Hervouet, friendly and chatty as ever. "You look radiant, Wendy," he says. His English is so quick I wonder how his French could be quicker. It is. We promise to stop by his shop later.

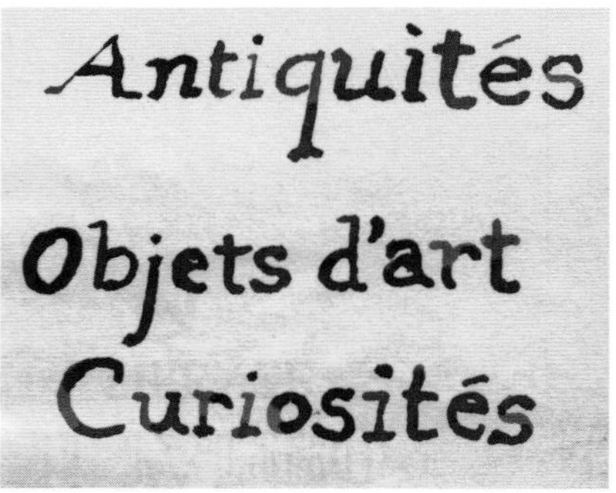

Antique stores are open late. They are most inviting at dusk, when appetites stir. We ring the bell of Galerie Hervouet. "Would you like a Scotch?" Jacques asks. In a flash he's back with a tray of drinks from the café next door. He tells us about an old Rolls he had. "It was pale blue. My son Augustin loved it. We kept it in a garage across the street from here."

Jacques shows us a cabinet of curiosities, about the size of a telephone booth, with drawers and shelves full of bird nests and butterflies and books. "It came from a country house."

"You can't get that on the plane," Wendy says to me.

"I could get it on a ship."

When Wendy admires a large wooden nautilus shell, Jacques offers it to her as a gift. I show him a catalog of my nature drawings. "Would you like to have an exhibition in my gallery?" he asks.

You never know who might be sitting next to you in Paris. One night at Le Voltaire a husky-voiced Lee Radziwill is a table away, the next morning at Café de Flore a beautiful transvestite smiles and takes a seat next to us. In Anahi, the Argentinian steak place on rue Volta, Francis Ford Coppola eats with a napkin tucked into his shirt.

Across from Sarah and me on the Métro one afternoon are two identical twin brothers in their late forties with identical bleach blond hair and chic, dark suits. They read the same newspaper, cross the same leg. Are they performance artists? In public, unknown wants to be noticed, known wants to be unnoticed.

Days are clear and mild, with spells of light rain and chill to remind us that it's winter. The blue skies are welcome, but don't seem quite right. Paris in winter is most itself when the sky is low and gray and sun nowhere to be found. Streets are more wistful and private, colors are deeper, wine better.

Wendy, Sarah, and I walk one fine day across Place du Carrousel to the Musée des Arts Décoratifs. "It's a small world even in Paris," Brad says as we cross paths in the

Tuileries. We ask him to join us. He falls in step, telling us as we go, about his visit to Villa Savoye, outside Paris. Brad, a landscape architect, likes that the Le Corbusier-designed house has a flat roof for a garden. "The size of the house was determined by the turning radius of a 1927 Citroën."

At the museum it's bags, bags, bags. Hundreds of "sacs," fancy and simple, from cultures old and new, fill the museum's huge vitrines. A Nigerian soothsayer's beaded bag, examples of the 18th-century French *reticule*, a 19th-century bag from England with an antislavery poem on its side. Material, shape, and function vary, but all are stylish in some way. There's a leather plumber's case, Bogart's Hermès bag, a fish bag by Christian Lacroix.

"I like the *furoshiki*," Wendy says, referring to the Japanese squares of cloth folded into a tote or purse that carries lunch, a gift, or in the old days, clothes to the public bath.

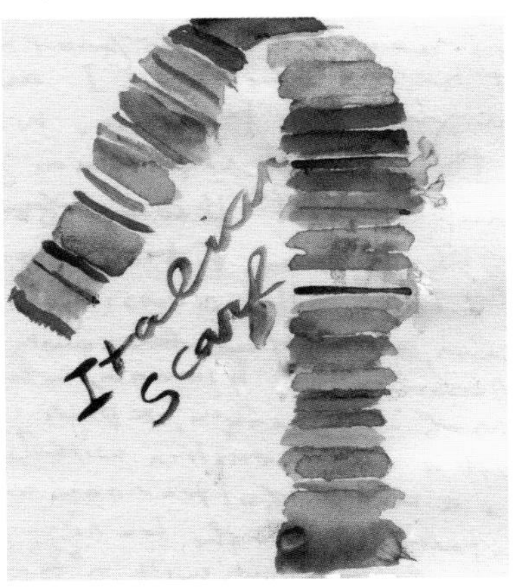

Speaking of style, even meter maids and firemen in Paris have it. They wear blue uniforms with red stripes. On the fire brigade's barge, tied up on the Seine, firemen scramble about in navy sweaters with a bright red *Pompier de Paris* across the chest. Police are sharply turned out.

The Republican Guard, who keep an eye on the Senate in Jardin du Luxembourg, wear navy jackets with circling white stripe, and blue kepis striped in red at the crown. Smart uniforms help relieve boredom. Guards at the Élysée Palace sport helmets with sprouting red bristles. Standing at parade rest with few passersby to glance at, they must find it hard to stifle a yawn. But they look good.

Antoine pours glasses of the strong house digestif after the meal. "*Les pruneaux*," he says. "*La reçette de mon grand-père. Bonne pour dormir.*"

"*Bon pour le scooter*," Sarah says and shudders.

It's Wendy's last night. "I won't see you for six months," Sarah says, putting her head on her mother's shoulder.

"Dad will be here another week."

"I met a boy today whose nickname is *Le Poulpe* because he puts his arms around everyone. His father is from Vietnam, his mother is Basque. He gave me some jars of her homemade *foie gras.*"

"What is *le poulpe*?"

"The octopus."

Wendy leaves. Sarah is out with new friends or emailing old ones. I worry about her being alone in Paris. "I'm going to be fine Dad." Her French is improving. She has a good accent and plunges in. A friend from New York takes her to the shows during Fashion Week.

I am alone in Paris. The best thing to do when you're on your own is to go to a bookstore. I visit the cramped Shakespeare and Company, picking up some classics for Sarah: *Down and Out in Paris and London, Birds of America, The Autobiography of Alice B. Toklas*. Later, wandering in the 6th, I discover the excellent Village Voice on rue Princesse, whose

silk +
bamboo
plane

1897

shelves and tables are stacked with contemporary books in English. I wish we had more good bookstores at home.

Hanging from the ceiling of a lobby in a building in the 3rd is a 130-year-old airplane made of silk and bamboo. It has wide, bat-like wings, three skinny bicycle wheels with metal spokes, and two sets of gangly propellers. The Avion III was created by Clément Ader in the 1880s and crashed almost immediately on its maiden flight. Restored in the 1980s, the marvelous craft is more whimsical sculpture than machine built to defy gravity. It is the perfect welcome to the Musée des Arts et Métiers.

The museum is full of scientific invention, much of it, like Foucault's fulcrum, which showed that the earth does indeed rotate, central to technological progress over the centuries. Nimbly engineered and constructed, many of the objects are works of art. Pascal's calculating machine from 1642, the Jacquard loom, Volta's battery, the Lumière brothers' cinematograph are here. The first steam-powered car, dating back to 1770, achieved a speed of two miles an hour. There are early clocks, microscopes, telephones, printers, designs for bridges, and scores of instruments and tools.

The place is a tinkerer's delight, a fabricator's utopia. Most of the collection is housed in the 11th-century priory of Saint-Martin-des-Champs. The museum honors the religion of science and the capacity of the human mind to find its way in the darkness.

A man hustles about with a tray of mint tea. He deposits a glass on your table in exchange for two euros. Birds flit about the patio. The Grand Mosquée de Paris is a peaceful place. Sarah joins me after a visit to the *hammam*

and we go into the café.

"How was it?" I ask.

"Have you ever been pummeled by a large, sweaty woman?"

"Can't say that I have."

"Are you familiar with *gommage*?"

"Is that like homage?"

"It's an exfoliant. Gets the dead skin off."

"Nice."

The table in the café is a round brass tray. The ceiling is carved cedar, tiles are all around. Sarah sits on a cushioned banquette. Gray light seeps through tall, arched windows. We order chicken couscous. "Remember that restaurant in Fes? La Maison Bleue?" I ask Sarah.

"I remember getting henna tattoos on my hands in the medina, and the kids in that little school room we went into, and all the sad donkeys."

"Pastry?"

"No thanks. I feel like a piece of dough myself. All that kneading and rubbing."

We finish our tea and walk through keyhole doorways into the mosque's walled garden. More tiles. The flowerbeds are empty. "Paradise," I say. "Islamic gardens are called paradise. They have walls around them. 'Para' means around."

"I'll have to come back when the garden is in bloom."

"And to get some more of that *gommage*."

We take the train to Versailles to get out of the city for a day. I haven't visited Versailles in twenty years and Sarah barely remembers going there as a child. It's a forbidding place, starting with the public entrance, a long cobbled incline to a big statue of Louis XIV. A place of preening (the beauty of the Hall of Mirrors redeems the hall somewhat) and pride in conquest (the Hall of Battles contains over thirty paintings of France at war ((mostly of Napoleon at war)). Vanity, power, pomposity, old French words. And American ones.

They still serve frog legs in Paris. Michel Troisgros, the chef at La Table du Lancaster, has the family way with food. His *cuisses de grenouilles* are sautéed and served in a tamarin sauce. The Chinese ate the first frog leg, it is said. The Chinese also consumed snails, as did the Romans. Pliny the Elder writes that snails, lettuce, eggs, and cold wine make a pretty good meal. Though now considered a delicacy, snails appear more often than frog legs on a Paris menu. The French eat forty thousand tons of escargot a year.

At the end of the meal the maître d' escorts the chef to our table. He is taken with Sarah. I tell him how much I enjoyed the frog legs. With a nifty side step he comes to my chair and beams with gratitude.

In the crypt of the Bibliothèque Nationale is a small exhibition of the striking set and costume designs of André Barsacq. He is unknown to me. As head of Théâtre de l'Atelier for over thirty years, he directed many plays and had an active career in film. He worked with Antonin Artaud, Jean-Louis Barrault, and Jean Anouilh. Barsacq with his wide-ranging talent reminds me of Dominique Serrand.

I think of the set Wendy and I designed with Dominique at the Guthrie Theater ten years ago. The play, *The Triumph of Love* by Marivaux, was directed by Dominique. It was set in a garden. We covered the proscenium stage with real grass and artificial topiary and ran water around the edge in a canal. The backdrop was a panoramic blowup of a blue and green abstract landscape I painted, inspired by the ethereal woods and sky of a Watteau painting. The crew had to take the pieces of sod on and off the stage every few days and set them outside in the summer sun.

Dominique and his fellow Parisian Vincent Gracieux (both dear friends) were awarded France's l'Ordre des Arts et des Lettres for their extraordinary work at Théâtre de la Jeune Lune, based in Minneapolis. We met them after attending one of their first plays in Minneapolis over thirty years ago. Dinners at our house became a weekly ritual. On Monday nights (when the theater was dark) friends and members of the troupe would gather in our kitchen.

Dominique would man the stove, managing to keep cigarette ash from falling into frying pans. Vincent cut cheese and sausage and smoked cigarettes. Wendy made a tart while I lit a grill in the snow. Bob and Katherine told funny stories, Barbra sliced and diced and laughed. Fred whacked the top off a bottle of champagne with a heavy knife. Chris played the piano, Josette sang. Not yet teenagers, David and Sarah loved it. They thought the circus had showed up in their living room.

At Chez Georges a beagle sniffs my leg, the man next to us rants in Czech, and brusque but motherly waitresses serve steaks and Béarnaise sauce with big bowls of *salade frisée aux lardons* and *céleri rémoulade.* The old French bistro never seems to die. A week ago in Aux Fins Gourmets Wendy overheard a sweet, wrinkled couple thank the shy, balding owner for keeping the place the same for so many years.

Paris is a place for nostalgists and lovers of old-fashioned places like Lasserre, where Sarah and I have our last dinner. Lasserre feels like a fancy nightclub in a 50s movie. It has pink walls and orchids, a piano player playing "La Mer," and an army of tuxedoed waiters serving silver-covered dishes. Best of all is the painted ceiling that opens to the sky. The restaurant may have grown fusty over the years (it dates back to the early 40s), but the food is good, and when the night sky appears above your head, you think Ezio Pinza will float down crooning "Some Enchanted Evening."

"Crêpe Suzette is on the menu," I say.

"My friend Laurent said Audrey Hepburn ate here," Sarah says.

"She studied at Parsons Paris, did you know?"

"She **did** not."

The Parsons "campus" is in the 14th. I go in the building briefly with Sarah and meet one of the administrators. A friendly, capable woman. While Sarah enrolls, I explore the neighborhood. Not far away is the Eiffel Tower. I walk down the Champs de Mars, along the Avenue Pierre-Loti. Dogs romp and children play under the pruned plane trees. A big Bernese mountain dog tugs on a leash held by a kind-looking elderly gentleman. A good sign. I look up at the tower rising in blue sky. I feel the pull of Paris all over again. It's good for Sarah to be here.

Sarah shows me her student I.D. "It's official," she says excitedly. "I met some of the other students. I liked them."

"I'm glad," I say, and give her a hug.

"I'm hungry. Let's have lunch.

2008

Our last night at the château we are given a tour of the cool, limestone cellar by Cédric, the short sommelier with the tall smile. He calls out vintages of the dusty bottles: "*Millésime 1925, millésime 1928.*"

"Any California wine?" David asks wryly.

The night is crisp and clear. We walk the crunchy paths through the lit topiaries to the small nude and the canal lined with beeches. We see stars and the lights of a plane blinking in the blue-black sky.

The entry into Paris through Porte Maillot and around the mad centrifuge of the Arc de Triomphe is itself a triumph. A biplane once flew through the arch, piloted by a Frenchman celebrating the end of World War I. Negotiating the circle by car may not be much safer.

"I think we will never get off the *périphérique,*" Wendy says. Down the Champs-Élysées, past the Ferris wheel on Place de la Concorde, across the Seine, and along the Boulevard Saint-Germain to Place de Furstenberg and rue Jacob.

Courtyard
12 rue Jacob

We are doors away from where Sarah lived as a student. Up a winding wooden staircase on the *premier étage,* our rented apartment wraps around one corner of a courtyard. Drop our bags and open the windows to the ancient chestnut trees and heavy cobblestones. Cobblestones, the unshed skin of Paris. Paris, the unbroken heart of the world.

I took a break from my notebook in 2006 and 2007, even though we came to Paris as usual. Didn't draw or write. I regret it now. Capturing things at the moment is a lot better than relying on one's rusty memory.

We rented our first apartment in 2006. We weaned ourselves from hotel breakfasts and concierges. We spoke French on the phone, stood in line to get a taxi, went to the grocery store and the market. The apartment was on rue de Verneuil in the 7th. We knew and liked the restaurants and cafés and shops in the neighborhood. And we liked being close to the river and on the Left Bank.

We bought bread and coffee and melons and had breakfast in the apartment. Wendy used the little red *Plan de Paris* less and less. We went farther afield in the city. With our own address, temporary though it was, we lived more like Parisians.

Sarah, still studying at Parsons, moved to rue Jacob, a block away from Place de Furstenberg. She locked herself out of her apartment one day and Alex, a friend who worked at La Palette two blocks away, carried a ladder from the café and climbed through an unlocked window. She fell in love with Ulysse, a Cavalier King Charles she adopted with a Paris friend.

David came from New York each year and we made the rounds of restaurants and cafés and museums. One night we heard Bono and the Edge sing "Happy Birthday" to a friend at dinner in Le Voltaire. In 2007, I had an exhibition of my drawings at Jacques Hervouet's gallery.

That year we stayed in an apartment on rue de Solférino, close to the Musée d'Orsay. At the end of the street a wooden pedestrian bridge crosses the Seine into the Tuileries. I often crossed the bridge in the early evening and walked in the gardens. In the waning light, the less crowded gardens seemed especially ancient and atmospheric.

In summer of 2006 a sculpture of Thomas Jefferson (in his hand a drawing of Monticello) was installed on the south side of the bridge. Each time I passed the tall bronze figure, going and coming, I looked up at him. I wanted to speak to him, or him to speak to me. Even a nod would have been enough, a silent affirmation that "yes, it's nice to be an American in Paris."

Saturday morning, the Puces de Vanves.

Wayward eyebrows above a ruddy nose. A Japanese woman's pale cheek. It's surprising how close in the jostling lanes your face comes to the faces of other flea market rummagers. It's cold and icy. A woman pushes her cart through the crowd. "*Thé, café, thé, café.*" Business is brisk.

Four dealers toss cards on a table, laughing, filling glasses with *vin du matin.* Every now and then one shrugs and pouts and calls out a price. We bargain for a small, unframed painting. The stretcher tacks are rusty, the paint a little cracked. There is a name in the corner. It's not Cézanne, but it's someone, someone who put down a bit of the world in color and with some charm.

at 12 rue Jacob
Sunday night
Fire in the Blood

Sarah calls Ulysse the little prince. David calls him a cat that barks. Sarah feels French when the Cavalier King Charles perches on her lap at the café. She took care of the dog while studying in Paris. "I want the prince to come home to L.A.," she says. A waiter brings a bowl of water for His Royal Lowness. When we leave, Ulysse blithely lifts his leg above the polished shoe of a man at one of the outside tables.

Tucked *en famille* into a paneled booth, we study the long, handwritten menu. The bust of Voltaire is half-hidden by a vase of flowers. Thierry tells us about his trip to Egypt. The puckish Antoine, whose family has owned the restaurant since before the war, tells us a slang word for sideburns. Sideburns are in vogue, the more Baroque the better.

"*Oh là là,*" says Pascal, presenting the *sole meunière* to Wendy before he filets it.

Excited about Barack Obama's success in the Iowa caucus, David spills wine on Sarah's jeweled blouse. "It's going to be an interesting campaign," I say.

"Yes, but what about my blouse?"

The Louvre's Cour Carrée is a vast stage at night with its floor of *pavés,* enfolding palace walls, and spare, elegant lighting. A couple enters through an arch, walking fast and gesturing grandly as if for an audience. A thin man stops in Hamlet thought near the middle of the cavernous space and searches through his coat pockets.

From the north end of Pont des Arts, we see the Eiffel Tower in the west. The hour turns and white lights shimmy up and down the tower. Across the Seine the gracious 18th-century Insitut de France glows more modestly. Paris enchants after dark because buildings and monuments are lit with care. On the wooden bridge young people drink and talk in the moth-gray light. Between the planks reflected lamplight plays on the surface of the water.

Standing in front of Fragonard's *Tête de vieillard* (Head of an Old Man), admiring the painter's nimble brushwork, I wonder when one becomes an old man. I just turned sixty.

Courbet at the Grand Palais. He was a bit of a wild man. He was accused of plotting to destroy the column in Place Vendôme. "I have to live like a savage," he wrote. "I have embarked on the vagabond life of the Bohemian." He made some wonderful paintings, lush and awkward, very unlike Fragonard. The wine-sleepy women on the bank of the Seine is on view and the gynecological *L'Origine du monde.*

Jo, the Beautiful Irish Girl, a portrait of Whistler's mistress, reminds me of Wendy.

David and Choghakate, a lovely young Armenian woman who is studying art in Paris, find a painting in the Louvre by the "Master of the Female Half-Lengths," the subject of Wendy's college thesis.

Sarah says, after a trip to Le Bon Marché with a friend, that she gets better service when Ulysse is with her. "Sales people love him. So do old ladies. They bend down and talk to him as if he's a baby. '*Bonjour, mon petit Cavalier King Charles. Bonjour, mon petit mignon.*'"

A man stops at our table in an Italian restaurant on rue du Cherche-Midi. "This must be the Coggins family." Wendy and I have no idea who he is. David introduces us. It's William Boyd, the celebrated British writer, a friend of David's from his London days. He and his wife are on their way back to London from their house in southern France. David has been trying to meet up with him, and now here he is.

"This is one of our favorite restaurants," Will says. "How did you know?"

Sunday morning, the sun breaks through. The fresh orange juice, dispensed by a clever machine at the Marché Biologique on Boulevard Raspail, is delicious. Ulysse sneezes at rotting lettuce on the wet ground while Wendy and Sarah pile hot roasted chicken, cheese, and tart in a basket for Sunday lunch at rue Jacob. The view of the courtyard from the dining room window goes well with market food and wine. We nap in the Old World way. Ulysse, at rest at last next to Sarah on the sofa, emits toy wheezes.

Place
Fürstemberg
Sarah et
Ulysses après
le marché biologique

The small, bright rink in front of city hall is filled with *les patineurs.* Couples and children holding cones of cotton candy glide and stumble around the crowded ice. Tall Africans skate with the speed of hockey players. One crashes accidentally into a woman, sending her to the hard ice flat out and probably to an emergency room. We hear the wail of a siren, as, shaken, we walk away.

We happen upon Epiphany vespers in Saint-Gervais church. We sit in cane chairs as a cappella voices, incense, and the arms of the devout rise in the cold air. The church in the Marais dates back to the 4th century.

François Couperin, court organist and composer for Louis XIV, got his start playing organ at Saint-Gervais. Couperin was a brilliant harpsichordist and composed hundreds of Baroque chamber works. In World War I a shell from a German weapon, called the "Paris Gun," crashed through the roof of the church. It was Good Friday. There were many dead and wounded.

We walk by the medieval houses nearby on rue François-Miron, an old Roman road. The half-timbered walls have survived war and fire and decay for almost a thousand years. Who knows what will survive? Or who? The Saint-Gervais organ built in the 17th century survived the bombing. People still play and listen to Couperin's music.

Our annual lunch at Le Grand Véfour begins with the walk through the Palais Royal in our "fancies." Wendy wears her silver shoes with ribbons around the ankle. They have been referred to in the family as "Dolly Parton" shoes.

The transition from the smoky *allées* of bare trees, to the restaurant's wine-dark banquettes and painted glass, is like stepping from a Bruegel into a Manet. Christian David, the silky maître d', shows us to our table. "*Bienvenue, bienvenue,*" murmurs the waiter with the basso profundo voice. The bespectacled waiter pours champagne with his usual bemusement. Menus, like holy tablets, are presented. At a certain moment in the long afternoon, time stops. The food, the laughter, the light become music.

The Palais Royal trees are spectral in the lilac evening. The lamps are on in the arcades. "I still can't believe you ordered wild pigeon," I say to Wendy. We are in front of the shop with the vintage dresses.

"Well, at least it wasn't *queue de boeuf*," she says looking at David.

"It was fantastic," David says.

"I love the *chariot de fromage*," Sarah says. "It's a meal in itself."

"Liebling wouldn't agree. It's just another course."

Like figures in a secret pageant, the sumptuous dresses of Chanel, Balenciaga, Saint Laurent, and Lagerfeld shimmer in the dark galleries of the Musée des Arts Décoratifs. Teenage students sit on the floor with pencils and drawing pads. Christian Lacroix organized the exhibit. His designs are feminine, intricate, and lavish.

"Here are dresses by Jacques Heim," Wendy says to me excitedly. "Remember, I wore his dresses in college."

"You wore Jacques Heim. I wore Levi Strauss."

The Marché aux Timbres is a good place to go if you are feeling nostalgic, and when are you not in Paris? Quiet men put boxes of old stamps, letters, and postcards on tables in the Carré Marigny. It's near the Élysées Palace. David and I like the florid addresses in fountain pen ink on cards of pre-war ocean liners and thin *Par Avion* envelopes, empty of letters. The postmarked stamps from the empire's outposts in Africa (Morocco, Senegal, Mozambique) and the Caribbean (Guadeloupe, Martinique) are more poignant for being obsolete.

"Nobody writes like that anymore," David says.

"Nobody writes by hand anymore."

"Except maybe old colonialists."

The *boudin noir* on the charcuterie plate at Le Comptoir gives a moment's pause before David digs in. A smartly dressed, cultivated man about New York, he doesn't appear to be the gourmet he is. A gifted writer, David wouldn't mind a job writing about travel and food, say in the manner of R. W. Apple, one of his heroes.

Each morning in monogrammed, white pajamas (a Christmas gift from a female admirer), he opens his computer to the home page of *The New York Times.* The light of the laptop, like the caveman's fire, never dies when he is in the apartment.

David talks politics and sports with equal fervor and knowledge. He watches football playoffs late at night in an English pub with an American Airlines pilot from South Dakota. He smokes cigars and does the *Herald Tribune* crossword, often with Sarah, always to the last letter.

"Sarah's got the dog, you've got the hat," he says about my new fedora.

"What's a five-letter word for weights abroad?" Sarah asks. "Oh . . . kilos."

"We're adding kilos to our weights abroad," David says.

"Just say no," I say.

"No to what?" Wendy says.

"Foie gras and crème fraîche."

"Foie gras maybe, crème fraîche never," Sarah says.

The January sales are in full swing. Saturday evening, the shops and streets of Saint-Germain-des-Prés practically vibrate with material longing. Cinderellas pull on slippers behind glass windows, shopping bags bump on the narrow sidewalks, cafés are kindergartens of bliss. Sarah's signature piece this season is a hat – a big white wool pile she wears at a sharp angle – and when dressing up, a purple sequined coat appropriated from her mother.

Fashion you buy, style you possess. Sarah has style to burn as does Wendy, but they don't mind spending a euro or two on fashion. A cheering mix of beauty and high spirits, Sarah makes friends (she has many here) and turns heads fast and faster. And she speaks French. She's a perfect ally in Paris. One waiter twirls like Fred Astaire and kisses her hand. "*Tu es belle, tu es belle,*" he gushes. Another, an Italian, whispers to me, "Can I marry your daughter?"

After dinner, David's last, Wendy and Sarah take a taxi from Hôtel George V to rue Jacob. David and I walk. He figures his cigar will last the distance. It's after midnight, and mild, and we have the sidewalks to ourselves. The lights of the Eiffel Tower and the Ferris wheel burn.

"Does Paris exist for Parisians or for tourists?" I ask. "Is it just a gorgeous amusement park? The Ferris wheel makes me want to say yes."

"The city still has its character, its soul," David said.

"Do you think so?"

"Yes, definitely."

"Good."

As we cross the Seine, I look at Place de la Concorde. The Ferris wheel is dark.

"Do you know you look like Goethe?" Wendy says, looking at a large plaster bust on a pedestal near the entrance of the museum.

"Interesting. We do have the same forehead. Too bad we don't have the same brain."

Ferdinand Hodler is one of Switzerland's great painters, and little did we know, significantly influenced the course of modern art. Until today, winding through a large exhibition at the Musée d'Orsay, we were not very familiar with his work. His symbolic paintings are strong in color and emotion: the seascapes with their simple symmetries are indeed strikingly modern, his portraits brutally honest.

In *The Night,* a monumental autobiographical painting from 1890, a man (Hodler) is wakened from sleep by a kneeling, shrouded figure representing death. Around him, in a bleak landscape, are other sleeping figures, including on one side of him his first wife, and on the other his lover who gave birth to his son. Hodler aligned the horizontal figures symmetrically, following the principle of parallelism, on which he based much of his work. He believed that repetition is the foundation of nature and that it gives work power and timelessness.

When *The Night* was banned in Switzerland as being obscene, Hodler showed it privately, and with the money he pocketed in entrance fees, took off for Paris, where reaction to his work was better.

What is this infatuation with the past?

A hundred years ago the tiny gallery now at 12 rue de Seine was a frame shop. I can detect it in a grainy, color photograph taken of the rue de Seine in the early 20th century. Delectable autochromes of that charmed Paris cover the walls of an exhibition in the Hôtel de Ville. I get up close to them, trying to feel what it was like to be in that square or this, buying flowers from the girl next to her wagon, or wine in that café.

Of course, the city then was not faded and dreamy as it is in the photographs; it was chaotic and raw, the dirt streets thick with horse dung. Maybe it's today's world that sends us back to the past, or here each year to the heart of Paris where everything seems to evoke the past, to value the past over the present. Was life better or more beautiful then? Paris is plenty beautiful now.

The old-fashioned Musée de la Chasse et de la Nature is trying to join the modern world. Once the slightly musty rooms of this gracious *hôtel particulier* in the Marais contained only trophy game and period furniture. Contemporary installations and sculptures now mix it up with the fancy rifles and stuffed animals. Some of the new additions are whimsical and tweak the old, some are didactic ("Stop destroying nature," one piece shouts). The many sweet François Desportes paintings and drawings of animals are untouched, thank god.

Suffering from too many late nights, Sarah huddles under the duvet at rue Jacob. Wendy offers motherly love and a plate of pasta. We take a break from our study of French gastronomy, but not for long. Two days later, to work up an appetite, we visit the Fondation Cartier in the 14th. Art has a tough time competing with Jean Nouvel's glass jewel of a building. Chandeliers of beads and bangles by Lee Bul, a South Korean artist, seem tailor-made for the setting. Robert Adams's photographs of clear-cut Oregon forests downstairs are depressing.

ANTIQU

Dessert at lunch is lychees and *fraises des bois.* The lychees are served skin on. You have to peel off the rough, red rind. The white flesh is sweet and perfumey. The *fraises des bois* come with a big bowl of crème fraîche.

Wendy and Sarah go their way while I pay a visit to the Gallimard bookstore on rue de Rivoli and farther down Galignani, which claims to be the first English bookstore on the continent. Galignani is like Pierre Hermé's bakery, but it's not creamy *macarons* you indulge in, rather lavish picture books rarely seen in the U.S.

The Tuileries in mist at sunset is a perfect setting for the familiar triad of reverie, melancholy, and fatigue. Back at rue Jacob, Wendy opens the windows. The ringing of church bells circles the courtyard and rises into our rooms like caroling birds.

"Is *rétroisme* a French word?" I ask Vincent. "You could use it to describe Aux Fins Gourmets."

"It's a little self-conscious," Vincent says. "But the nicotine stains on the walls are real."

"And the phone in the phone booth is real," Wendy says. "We've heard it ring."

"Was it for you?" he says and laughs his deep, barrel-chested laugh. Our old friend Vincent Gracieux recently moved back to his native Paris after working for thirty years in theater in America. He was married to Katherine Lanpher, the American writer and radio commentator. When we hear that laugh we know all is well.

"Of course, I miss my friends in America and I miss the old theater, but I'm happy," he says. "I am working with a good theater here with actors from all over the world. We tour Europe and Britain. *La vie en France est bonne, n'est-ce pas?*"

"Do you mind all the touring?"

"It keeps me young." The laugh.

We order the *boeuf bourguignon.*

We are lost in dark, rainy Bois de Vincennes. The taxi driver finally pulls up next to La Cartoucherie where the Footsbarn Theater is staging *L'homme qui rit* in a yellow tent. Vincent adapted the play from Hugo's novel and has a major role. Though the benches are hard and our French is not good enough to understand everything, Wendy and I enjoy the inventive, highly visual production.

Afterward in a mobile café, we meet the director who is English and actors from Java and Japan. A large woman dressed in African garb serves wine and tea, smiles and chats with everyone. "Is she with the company?" I ask Vincent.

"No, she just works in the café."

"Do you know her name?" Wendy asks.

"Fanta."

We ride back on the Métro. A bit of leftover makeup under Vincent's eyes shines in the glaring subway light. *"À l'année prochaine,"* we say wistfully to Vincent and give him a hug.

"Until next year," he says with a smile as he gets off the train. He bows quickly then walks away.

Friday night, the café levitates. We order a bottle of champagne. Sarah prepares for a long round of goodbyes – she leaves tomorrow for L.A. I think back to our lavish dinner at Le Cinq on David's last night, when Wendy in her endearing, inimitable way, told her children across the white table and the forest of wine glasses that she loved them.

The drawings of Polidoro da Caravaggio, an obscure, talented student of Raphael's, are mounted in low light in the drawings cabinet of the Louvre. This small, scholarly show of Madonna and child, and classical myth works (in sanguine and *pierre noire* and ink) requires some scrutiny. You can take your time and move freely, unlike negotiating the crowds breathing heavily around the *Mona Lisa* or the *Victory of Samothrace.*

We make our ritual pilgrimage to the Italian galleries. The pink and green swatches of the Siennese school, the small Pisanello portraits of prince and princess, the sad, masculine faces of Duccio's Madonnas, the Fra Angelico frescoes, the Giotto fragments, the mesmerizingly modern Uccello battle scene.

These familiar works are in a way like touchstones. Apart from their aesthetic power and their place in art history, they do what all great works of art do – they restore to you your sense of awe. They make you feel intensely human and glad to be alive. That they have been preserved and protected over centuries, and are now here for us, for the world, to see and take sustenance from, is nothing short of miraculous.

With his inverted eyebrows, half-closed eyes, and famous grin, he is instantly recognizable. He apologizes for putting his wide body between our table and his as he slides

TAXI
PARISIEN

Paris

au Musee de
la Vie Romantique

into the banquette to join a French couple for dinner. He helps himself to our carafe of "Paris" water. "It's warm in here, isn't it?" He orders steak au poivre, profiteroles, and Coke. He talks about collecting art and his movies: *Batman, Chinatown,* and the two Jakes. The French woman asks him something about the "Cuckoo Nest" film. He puts on his sunglasses and waves broadly to no one in particular when he leaves.

The Musée de la Vie Romantique is a small quaint house in the 9th that celebrates the life of George Sand and the art of Ary Scheffer, who lived there in the 19th century. "I care only for those things that belonged to people I loved," Sand said. Among the items on display are her jewelry, her watercolors, and the many portraits artists made of her.

Place Pigalle is seedy and lively like a racy, unkempt friend. We haven't been here in a long time. Not much has changed. Bars, guitar shops, and sex clubs. Men take money from tourists gullible enough to play games of chance and trickery. The long hike up to Sacré-Coeur on *butte Montmartre* is worth it for the view. This is the highest point in the city. A young crowd sits and sways on the steps in front of the bone-white basilica. Boys play guitars and sing Bob Marley songs. Paris lies before them wide and inscrutable.

We cross the Seine on the Pont des Arts. It's midnight. The hour changes and the Eiffel Tower lights up. We walk along the river next to the Louvre and cross back over on Pont Royal. Down rue du Bac to rue de l'Université looking in the antique shops. We go into the café and sit down in one of the red banquettes.

"Yes, I know," the waiter says. "Two Cognacs."

212

2009

France is white with snow and blue with cold. A man named Guillaume drives us into the city from CDG, testing our knowledge of Paris museums along the way. "Do you know the Musée Gustave Moreau? Have you been to the Maison de Victor Hugo? The museum of dolls, of magic, of the post?"

We are staying at 6 rue de l'Abbaye in a grand apartment on the fifth floor overlooking the paulownia trees of Place de Furstenberg and an expanse of rooftops that spread to the towers of Notre-Dame. Pigeons and gulls wheel and dip outside the immense arched windows. There are four bedrooms, three baths, a stairway leading to a loft beneath the mansard roof, and a wall of Gallimard editions around a marble fireplace in the vast, flesh-colored living room. The more modest apartment we had originally booked on rue Jacob became unavailable suddenly, and we were given this lavish place instead.

We meet Vincent at La Palette and catch up over wine and *tartines*. Still with Footsbarn Theater, he leaves Paris soon to begin touring. "I am so happy Barack Obama won," he says. "I am not so happy about the economy. And the cold." He rubs his hands together. "It's hard to smoke outside."

All of Europe is frigid. Bulgaria has little or no heat because of a lack of natural gas from Russia (withheld for political reasons), causing an international uproar. Fewer Americans are on the prowl, but the chilly streets are full of Parisians in floppy-eared, fur-lined hats and tangles of scarves.

David arrives the day after we do. We walk along the river to Le Voltaire. Amid the customary, high welcome and *bonne années,* we discover that Antoine, the smiling *maître de déférence* whose family has owned the restaurant on the Quai Voltaire for decades, is really a chef, and shedding tux for toque, is back in the kitchen. Stephanie, his fiancée (another surprise), has taken over the front of the house.

David and I share a pheasant roasted in Antoine's oven. Wendy has the truffle salad. "I've been waiting all year for this." The small, wood-paneled dining room, like a small train car really, purrs with an elegant and pampered crowd. Every table is full; there is only one seating.

David spent New Year's in Connecticut with Duncan Hannah and Megan Wilson and other New Yorkers. "I cooked dinner," he says. "*Pot-au-feu* with beef from a cow raised by Sam Waterston."

"You mean Jack McCoy?" Wendy says.

"He's a cattleman," David says.

"How did it turn out? The *pot au feu?*"

"Everything was in order."

David and I take a train from Gare du Nord to Brussels, then to Ghent, to see van Eyck's 15th-century altarpiece in St. Bavo's Cathedral. A lady selling gingerbread points in the direction of the church as we slip and slide across the icy square. Jan's brother Hubert started the extraordinary piece, but Jan took over and finished it after Hubert died. A shy Adam and a paunchy Eve in the side panels are almost life-size and so real they could be town hippies. A stuffy British voice on the audio phone tells us about the controversy over whether God or Christ sits in the upper central panel, and that thirty-seven identifiable flowers bloom in the field around the blissful, bleeding lamb.

jane

David goes to the studio of Michaël Booremans, the Belgian painter, to interview him for *Art in America.* We meet later in Bruges, where we stay the night. The canals are frozen, the dogs sweatered, the pubs full. In one place you can consume all the brown bread and cheese you want but only three steins of the strong 13th-century Trappist ale. We shiver from church to museum to church, thawing a little in front of morbid, highly finished Flemish paintings, before catching a late train to Paris. We ride back silently, looking out at the trees in the fields covered in hoarfrost beneath a full moon.

Brasserie Lipp, Saturday night. The banquettes teem with faces, craggy, saggy, lifted, tanned. Talking, laughing, whispering, posing. Hair is wild, coiffed, depleted. Jewels are outsized, dogs pint-sized. Plates of sausage and potatoes and raw steak and oysters line waiters' arms like trophies. Tabletops are miracles of composition; everything fits, pots of mousse, wine glasses, demitasses, cell phones. It's loud, bustling theater under the most glaring of lights. Everyone in the place looks as if she just stepped from a stage or from in front of a lens, including the stony maître d' who looks like Jean Reno.

The waiter puts a chocolate pastry garnished with gold in front of me. "Compliments. *C'est feuille d'or. Pour le roi.*" Another is placed in front of Wendy. "*Pour la reine.*"

We ride up to the fifth floor in the narrow wooden elevator with two black ornate metal doors. "*Fermez la porte doucement et complètement s.v.p.*" Inside the apartment, we open the window for fresh air. Footsteps echo up from the street. There is distant laughter and singing. It's a different world, removed, serene. Nothing above but the night sky.

Next morning a hammer sounds, then a saw. I open the kitchen door to the back stairway and find a man carrying lumber. A garret space is being turned into an apartment. *"Je suis désolé,"* he says. *"C'est la vie dans la ville."*

During the day an elderly man sits at his desk in an apartment across the square. His room is filled with shelves of books. He writes, talks on a telephone, meditates. A scholar in solitude. One morning two men in a cherry picker perch high outside our window and slice, with a chain saw, branches from the paulownia trees.

The sound of church bells floats above hurrying Parisians, loitering tourists, the homeless man with his blanket and cell phone. We have breakfast in the living room, before the big window. Wendy goes out every morning for fresh bread, fresh juice, a newspaper. Mornings are leisurely. It's hard to leave the queen's aerie.

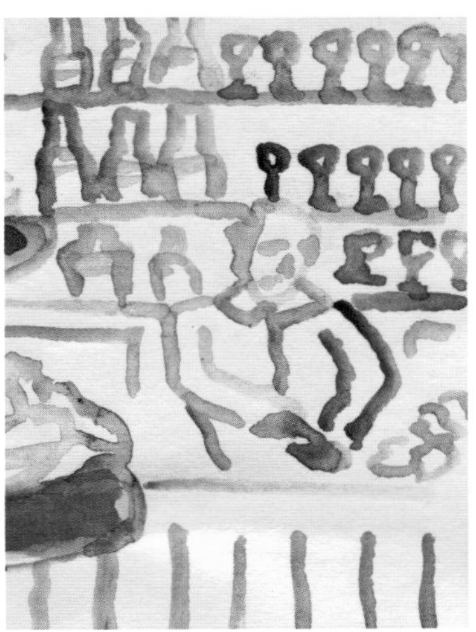

At Saturday lunch on the café side of Le Voltaire, Antoine appears in his whites, like a chef Pierrot, and talks about his cooking exploits with Taillevent, Alain Ducasse, and other restaurants. He shows Wendy the truffle slicer he uses to slice the paper-thin mushrooms on her salad. "You must use firm mushrooms."

We stop at the Village Voice bookstore and chat with Odile, the owner. I met her last year when she took copies of *The Nostalgic Heart,* my travel memoir about cities, for her shop. "Amazon is not good for my store," she says. "Nor is the Kindle." I pick up a small book by John Berger called *The Red Tenda of Bologna.*

"Nothing can replace a real book," Wendy says.

"And a good bookseller," I add.

The grand gallery of the Louvre is lined with paintings beguiling as courtesans at court. Off the hall is the queen herself, the *Mona Lisa.* Around the corner in the same room is Titian's *Le Concert Champêtre,* one of my favorite paintings. A city boy strums a lute for his country cousin in a sylvan wood. He sings, perhaps, of pleasures behind the walls of the town in the background. Or maybe he wants to know if life is more fun in the country. There is an intimacy between them. The two statuesque nudes are not real. They are there to show what's on the boys' minds. They represent pleasure.

Across from the *Mona Lisa* is Paolo Veronese's thirty-foot wide painting, *The Wedding Feast at Cana.* Centerstage at the large banquet (which incudes Mary and Jesus) is Veronese himself, in white, playing the viola da gamba. He is accompanied by Titian, in brilliant red, also playing

an instrument. Various members of European royalty in sumptuous attire are gathered around the tables, or so it is thought. A turbaned Suleiman the Magnificent looks ill at ease. Thick, white clouds hover in a blue sky behind a distant campanile. Columns, pink and white, rise above the feasting crowd.

Mary and Jesus sit at the main table. He has just performed the miracle of turning water into wine. A man in an elegant robe studies his newly filled glass. Dogs lounge in the foreground, while behind the balustrade above Jesus a man butchers a lamb.

The painting has a checkered history. It hung in the Benedictine Monastery of San Giorgio Maggiore in Venice for over two hundred years until Napoleon decided he wanted it. It was cut in half and sewn back together in Paris. It suffered further indignity in World War II when it was rolled up and hauled around France in a truck. And twenty years ago during a million-dollar restoration the canvas was torn in a number of places when the painting fell on the floor.

One evening at Café de Flore we meet Choghakate, the Armenian woman David often sees when he is in Paris. She is studying art and working in a gallery. "She bought me a beer," David says, "which I take as a good sign, because she doesn't drink."

"Does she like your new beard?" Wendy asks.

Later he writes that his meal on the plane to New York was described on the menu as "chicken with cheese inside." He remembers the poetic descriptions by Christian David of the dishes at Le Grand Véfour. "*La langoustine mitonné les légumes, la salade de jeunes pousses et truffes, le canard croise aux épices.*"

On his website, David posts a picture of the Normandie crossing the Atlantic, "the slow way back to New York." And one with better food.

The Jardin des Plantes was originally the Jardin du Roi. It was a garden of medicinal herbs planted for Louis XIII in the early part of the 17th century. Open to the public in 1640, it has grown to include a number of gardens, a labyrinth, a zoo, and several museums. It is lovely to stroll the long allées even in winter, pausing at the alpine garden or warming up in the huge greenhouse of tropical plants. Wendy and I wander through an exhibit of 18th-century botanical prints, part of an abandoned project to compile a book of the world's flowers.

To the south of the entrance is the Galerie de paléontologie et d'anatomie comparée. Guarding the venerable, brick building is a latter-day stegosaurus looking more wry than fierce. The museum is a long, open gallery of two floors and large arched windows. Standing more or less in rows across the wooden first floor is an army of skeletons of almost every vertebrate imaginable – dinosaurs, whales, rhinos, lions, birds.

They are frozen in 19th-century time, when they were collected and displayed by the scientists and explorers of the day. There are some thirty-six thousand specimens in the collection. The displays now look old-fashioned, but the museum was once of the highest level. The place is completely appealing to the amateur naturalist, to any boy or girl or aging soul who loves the natural world.

Sarah manages to get all her bags and herself in the tiny elevator. After a tour of the apartment, we get back in the elevator and go to La Palette. Jean-François, less hirsute, still holds forth at the café. "Welcome back to Paris. Where is your son?"

"Back in New York sadly," Wendy says.

"I wish bro were still here," Sarah says.

"He left some food behind," I say.

"I'm looking forward to some good meals."

"I need to give my stomach a rest," Wendy says. Indeed she takes to bed later in the day. Sarah and I shop in her old neighborhood on rue de Buci and haul food and bottles of water back to the apartment. Dinner Sarah's first night in Paris is *pasta chez nous*. She puts the water on to boil while Wendy sleeps.

The Hôtel de Soubise, a 14th-century mansion on rue des Archives in the Marais, is home to the Musée de l'Histoire de France. Samples from the immense French archives are on display. Wonderfully odd things, like a primitive drawing of a submarine (1689), the derringer used in the attempted assassination of King Louis-Philippe in the early 19th century (also a piece of the king's carriage where the bullet lodged), a video of Klaus Barbie's trial, and dossiers of Gustave Eiffel's request to change his name from Bönickhausen to Eiffel and Marc Chagall's to become a French citizen.

Deep boxes with marbled interiors, old documents and letters wrapped with string, dates and titles in florid handwriting. History may have been bloody and harsh, but its records and artifacts are preserved meticulously. Even the means of moving historical documents from one place to another was elegant. *Le crochet pour transport des boites d'archives* used in the early 20th century is a kind of backpack with wooden struts and leather straps and a shelf. Perfect for hauling boxes stuffed with vellum from the bowels of a palace.

Barack Obama is inaugurated as the forty-fourth U.S. president. We sit in the kitchen with a bottle of champagne and watch with tears and awe as he and his lovely wife, Michelle, and daughters, Malia, and Sasha, become America's first family. Several million people gather on the National Mall in the cold to watch Supreme Court Justice John Roberts administer the oath (with miscue) and Aretha Franklin sing "My Country, 'Tis of Thee" (with a tremendous gray bow on her hat). Michelle Obama holds a Lincoln Bible under her husband's hand.

The French woman who lives in the apartment across the hall shares the elevator with us. "It's a great day for you," she says. "I hope we won't be disappointed. Expectations are very high for Mr. Obama."

We stop by Jacques Hervouet's shop to say hello. He is levitating with joy after the ceremony. "Nine million people in France watched the inauguration," he says.

Wendy and I walk through the south pavilion and enter Place des Vosges. It's the oldest square in Paris and the most beautiful. It was built in 1605 by Henri IV, "the good king." A champion of art and religious tolerance, Henri IV accomplished much during his reign. He built Pont Neuf, the Louvre's grand gallery, and cleaned up state finances. He planted mulberry trees and introduced silkworms in the Tuileries with the idea of starting a silk industry. He strove for peace and prosperity and, as legend goes, a chicken in every pot. And it could be added, a king in every bed. He had so many mistresses, he was called *le vert gallant,* or the green gallant.

The uniformity and symmetry of Place des Vosges is stunning. Red brick buildings (some have real brick, some fake) with steep slate roofs and vaulted arcades line the perfect square (one hundred forty meters by one hundred forty meters). They enclose a garden of clipped lime trees, fountains, arabesque lamps, and an equestrian statue of Louis XIII, Henri's son. A people's place now, it was once the home of royalty. When her husband Henri II died in a tournament on the grounds, Catherine de' Medici had the château destroyed and moved to the Louvre.

We leave the square and walk by the 17th-century Hôtel de Sully. With its ancient courtyard and graceful walls it's always a pleasant surprise. The peaceful, private atmosphere of the Marais is somewhat ironic. It's so much of a neighborhood, yet it's so chic and historic. Outside the immense *hôtel particuliers* pass Parisians in tight sweaters and expensive shoes. The quarter is full of boutiques and cafés.

"Still too trendy for you?" I ask Wendy.

"A little but it's fun to walk here."

In one storefront is the workshop of the architect Renzo Piano. Walls are covered with wooden forms and metal tools. You can see models of his designs and the people making them. Young men sit at vast, messy tables focused like schoolchildren with crayons and paper.

Rain has replaced the cold and falls lightly on the narrow quiet streets. Newsstands are pasted with pictures of Michelle and Barack. A photo in the *Herald Tribune* shows the huge square in front of Hôtel de Ville filled with Parisians enraptured at the making of the new president.

Jacques Prévert was a man of many talents, as an exhausting and fascinating exhibition at the Hôtel de Ville makes abundantly clear. French curators are not a circumspect lot. Nor was Prévert. He was a surrealist poet, political activist, screenwriter of films including *Les Enfants du Paradis,* collagist, and friend and collaborator to writers and artists.

Clips from movies and documentaries play in niches set up like small theaters. One shows Yves Montand, young and handsome, singing "Les Feuilles Mortes," whose lyrics are from a poem by Prévert. (English lyrics to "Autumn

Leaves," an American pop classic, are by Johnny Mercer.) There are provocative collages made after Prévert suffered a stroke, books of poetry, original manuscripts, children's books, scores, photographs of him with Picasso, André Breton, Jean-Louis Barrault, art from his collection, art that he made. No stone is left unturned.

Early drafts of his screenplays are especially fetching. Large sheets of paper are filled helter-skelter with dialogue and ideas and small colorful drawings of characters and settings. Prévert's life was rich and full. Inside the crowded exhibition you can feel the affection for the man. Prévert is a hero in France.

One Saturday night before dinner we have champagne with Jacques and Adeline in the Galerie Hervouet. We sit amid the antiques and odd objects in sculpted stone chairs around a large table made of red wood. Sarah, radiant and effervescent, regales the French couple with tales of life in L.A.

There is talk of the election, of the Hervouet's recent trip to New York. "I love what you did in the window," Wendy says to Jacques. Old mirrors and paintings surround a peacock and decaying columns. Augustin, their young son, hides in the back room. "Gus," Jacques calls out, "come say hello."

On Sunday we all (minus Sarah) pile into the Hervouet's little Golf and drive to Adeline's family's country home in Saint-Léger, about forty-five minutes west of Paris. We stop first in Montfort-l'Amaury, a pretty stone village which includes among its attractions a château in ruins and the former home of Maurice Ravel. "Lots of Parisians have second houses here," Adeline says. We visit the cemetery, the church, and a favorite café where Augustin devours *pommes frites*. "Do you have *pommes frites* in the U.S.?" he asks.

Adeline's childhood home sits on the edge of the forest

and village of Rambouillet. It consists of an enlarged farmhouse, two houses the family rents out, a pond with an island where she and Jacques were married, and a large yard that was a playground of wild grass in Adeline's youth. Adeline makes lunch while Jacques lays a fire in the living room. He pours glasses of Scotch and vermouth. Augustin dashes off to the neighbors.

The dining room has been rewalled in boiserie and bird prints, overseen by Jacques and Adeline's father. After lunch and a walk in the forest (a key to the gate entering the forest hangs on a tree), we drive back in rain and heavy traffic to Paris. We talk about architecture. "Vaux-le-Vicomte is more beautiful and human than Versailles," Adeline says.

"The Institut de Paris is marvelous," Jacques says.

"The best of classical Paris. Did you know the Académie Française meets there to decide what goes into the French dictionary? They want to keep the language pure."

"Must be hard with all the English invaders," I say. "*Le top, le jogging, le snob.*"

"And *le beep,*" Wendy says, referring to the remote that opens the country house gate.

We go to Café de Flore and shake hands with the waiters and the suited maître d'. We order cognac and take in the late-night crowd. People write in notebooks, read, toss hair, discuss, gesture, kiss, look around. They are interested in the menu of people, not the menu of food and drink (ignored by regulars). It's men's fashion week. Pierre Bergé, longtime lover and business partner of the late Yves Saint Laurent, is sitting with an emaciated writer and actor with white bangs and piercing blue eyes. "*Il est très bien connu,*" the waiter says about the writer.

Sarah and Thomas join us. Thomas is a lawyer and comes from a highly cultivated French family. He is polite and engaging. "I am working on a book," he says.

"What is it about?" Wendy asks.

"Elvis."

"Presley?"

"Yes. I'm going to Memphis to do research." Thomas says in a mock Southern accent.

"He has already written a book about Bob Dylan," Sarah says.

"What did you think of Hibbing?" I ask.

"Sadly I did not get to Hibbing."

"Will you have Ulysse for the weekend?" Wendy asks.

"No," Sarah says and makes a sad face. "Christophe said I could, but now he's not sure. I bought a little, orange dog raincoat. I may get him for an afternoon."

"Maybe you need someone to negotiate for you," I say. "Someone who knows the language."

"Are you up on canine law?" Sarah asks Thomas.

"*Les lois pour les chiens?* No, unfortunately I am not. But I have a colleague...."

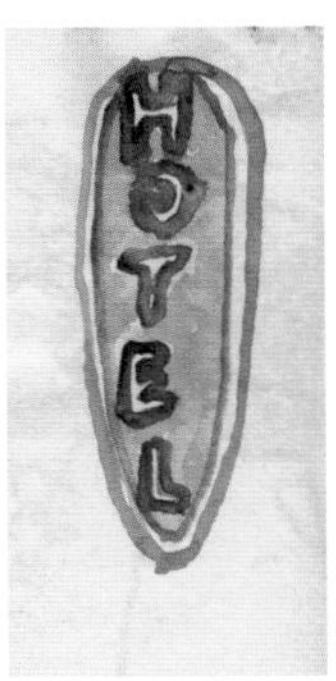

Does any serious contemporary painter paint the female figure? I mean in a sensual, more or less classical way? Lucian Freud and John Currin paint nudes, but they are hardly sensual. Is the odalisque as subject exhausted or just déclassé? Such questions arise while taking in the "Picasso et les Maîtres" exhibition at the Grand Palais.

In the last room of this elephantine show are Titian's *Venus with an Organist and with Cupid,* Goya's *The Nude Maja,* and Manet's *Olympia.* All sumptuous iconic nudes. It's jolting to see them hanging side by side on the same wall. It's quite the curatorial coup.

If it takes Picasso's overexposed work, which doesn't always stand up to the masters, to make this show possible, so be it. (Isn't it time to declare a moratorium on Picasso shows for awhile?) To see so many terrific works by pre-Picasso painters in one place is worth it even if you have to throw an elbow or two, and even if the theme of the exhibition is a little strained.

I always stop at La Librairie des Alpes to look at the clutter of items in the window. How does a bookstore devoted to books and ephemera on mountains manage to survive? The bearded bookseller in hat and scarf says hello. He's friendly; we talk. It's my first time in the shop. "You don't have to be an alpinist to come into the store," he says. I buy a book from the thirties of scenic Mont Blanc photos.

The *bouquinistes* have opened their boxes. Some sell Eiffel Tower key rings and "I Love Paris" magnets, but most maintain the traditional stock of second-hand books and botanical prints and vintage postcards. By law each box is two meters long and painted the dark green of old train cars. They've been around in some form since the 17th century and are still in demand. It takes years for a box to become available. Today they seem more aimed at the tourist, but I would miss them if they were not there. I would like to have a *bouquiniste's* box for my favorite books.

Of the thousands of bookstores in France, half it seems are in Paris. French celebrate writers as Germans celebrate composers as Americans celebrate celebrities. There are palatial museum bookstores full of richly illustrated books with titles like *The Hat in Medieval Art.* Shops with somber Gallimard books on politics and philosophy with clinical covers. Shops with little room to move, but lots of charm and second hands: Fitzgerald and Mann in French or the odd Graham Greene in classic orange Penguin.

There must be a dozen places devoted to English books, but there is also one for Polish books on the Boulevard Saint-Germain which has been around a century or more. There is, not surprisingly, Librairie Gourmande and La Musardine, an erotic bookstore. There is L'Harmattan, which has books on Africa, and La Librairie du Jardin, a narrow cave of a place just inside the Concorde gate of the Tuileries that has thousands of books on gardens.

Inspired by a passage in *Antoine's Alphabet,* Jed Perl's book about Watteau, I pick up a copy of Balzac's *Cousin Pons.* It's the story of a homely, doleful musician, a lover of food and paintings and antiques who comes to tragic end in the grasping, covetous world of 19th-century Paris. I read it at night when I can't sleep. I turn on the lamp in the empty bedroom with the flowered walls and the window overlooking the square. I'm almost happy to be awake. I slip under a blanket and open the book. Even insomnia in Paris has a pleasant side to it.

> *The excessive melancholy abounding in this poor man's pale eyes immediately struck anyone who might have mocked, and froze the jest on his lips. In a flash the thought came that nature had forbidden this man to make tender advances, because they could only awaken laughter or distress in a woman. A Frenchman is speechless when he meets that misfortune which in his eyes is the cruelest of all misfortunes: the inability to attract.*

Sunday night at Le Cherche Midi. The waiter refuses to clear Sarah's plate until she finishes her *fettucine al tartufo nero*. Sarah tells us about lunch with Thomas's grandmother. "Everybody in his family lives within a block of each other."

The tiny Italian restaurant on rue du Cherche-Midi is full. Mature, sophisticated couples finger unlit cigarettes, skinny men in space-age glasses talk fast, young men and women touch hands. One foppish man is adorned with a rather strange concoction: doll-like stuffed hands sticking out from his shirt collar. "Where did he get that idea?" Sarah says, raising an eyebrow.

"We saw Watteau's paintings today," I say. *Pierrot* and *The Embarkation for Cythera.* I love the *fêtes* paintings, the settings in the woods, the theatricality, the light-heartedness. But also the secrecy, the intimacy, and the..."

"And the melancholy. Or melancholia I should say," Sarah says.

"Have I talked about Watteau before?"

Sarah and Wendy look at each other.

"What would you say, Sarah? *Cent fois? Mille fois?*"

A cold, clear morning. Wendy and I wander through the green hills of Parc Montsouris in south Paris. It's in the 14th by the Cité Internationale Universitaire de Paris. It's our first time here. Paths wind and curve by thick beeches and sculptures, along faux wood railings and fences, around a large pond of quacking ducks. Lamps look as if they date from the creation of the park in 1869. Unlike the geometric Luxembourg Gardens or the Tuileries, Parc Montsouris, designed by Jean-Charles Alphand and Jean-Pierre Barillet-Deschamps, is organic and rambling. It's more like an English garden, more like the fantastical Parc des Buttes-Chaumont in the 10th, also designed by Alphand.

Baron Haussmann, the mastermind behind modern Paris, had a big hand in developing the city's parks. He asked Alphand and Barillet-Deschamps to create these verdant spaces for the city's growing population. Interesting that Haussmann, ruthless demolisher of the labyrinthine neighborhoods of medieval Paris in favor of wide, sterile boulevards and modern buildings, should favor such romantic designs.

Near the park are houses on narrow cobblestone lanes that run perpendicular to one another. Braque once had a studio in this neighborhood. A street sign reads *Rue Georges Braque 1882-1963 Peintre Cubiste.* Also nearby is Villa Seurat, a quiet dead-end street with a notable pedigree. A number of the houses were designed by the architect André Lurçat and were homes to artists and writers. Built in the 1920s, they have plain Art Moderne fronts with large, many-paned windows.

Villa Seurat is named after painter Georges Seurat, who may have lived here at one point in his brief life. Henry Miller wrote *Tropic of Cancer* while living at No. 18 near the end of the street. Anaïs Nin was his housemate.

Wendy once saw Salvador Dalí at the Hôtel Le Meurice. It was in 1967 in the glittering Restaurant Le Meurice, where she had gone with a college friend and her family for dinner. She tells the story again for Sarah. "He and his wife looked like an ordinary couple having dinner. Except for the moustache."

"Do you think Dalí would have been as successful without his sling of a moustache?" I ask. "And his bulging eyes?"

We are having lunch in Restaurant Le Dalí in the Meurice. It's our last day in Paris. We talk about visiting Sarah in California, about her work as a stylist, about Wendy turning sixty. The waiter who used to work at Hôtel Montalembert chats with Sarah in French.

The lobby restaurant has just been redesigned in high surreal style by the ubiquitous Philippe Starck, who happens to be sitting nearby at a table of Asian men in dark suits. He is dressed casually, and with him is his wife Jasmine. Starck has something of Dalí's impish showmanship and holds forth in oracular fashion.

"First Dalí, now Starck," I say to Wendy.

"Was Dalí's wife as lovely as Starck's?" Sarah asks.

The large room is full of Parisians and hotel guests, the quick and the dead. Chair arms are fish, lamps are branches. The ceiling is a vast canvas painted by Starck's daughter, Ara, of bronzed-colored figures leaping and dancing between theater curtains.

After lunch we stroll along rue Saint-Honoré. We stop in a store and buy a present for Sarah. The young woman who helps us is polite and patient in a way you don't often find in modern life. She wraps the scarf carefully in a monogrammed box and walks around the counter to present it to us. The art of luxury still has a place in our flattened, newly spartan world.

We walk through the Tuileries and across the river. The air is mild. The late afternoon light bathes the Louvre and the bridges and the river. We walk with coats open, shoulders spread. We walk past the *bouquinistes* and along the small garden at the end of rue de Seine. The sculpture of a wistful Voltaire stands in the garden. I punch in the code by the big door on rue de l'Abbaye. The lock clicks discreetly. We climb into the tiny wooden elevator and go up to the apartment.

2010

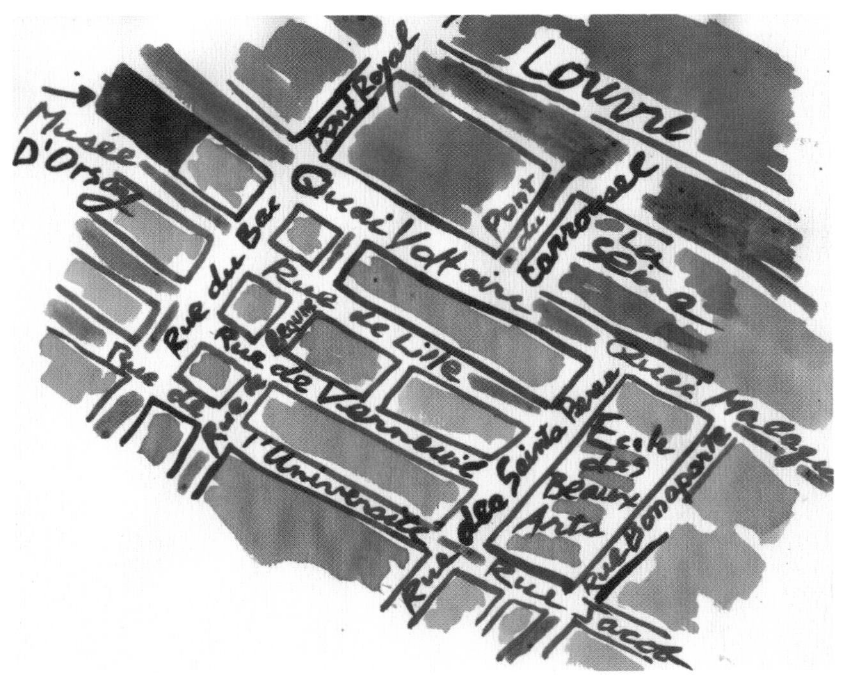

Musée D'Orsay
Pont Royal
Louvre
Quai Voltaire
Pont du Carrousel
La Seine
Rue du Bac
Rue de Lille
Rue de Verneuil
Quai Malaquais
Ecole des Beaux Arts
Rue des Saints Pères
Rue Bonaparte
Rue Jacob

"We thought you were Hubert de Givenchy," says the Frenchman sitting next to us at Le Voltaire. "Do you have some Irish in you?"

"Yes," I say. "Irish, English, and Scottish."

"So do I," he says shaking my hand.

One of the women at his table has a dachshund wearing a sweater with a dog bone embroidered on it. Ignored at its table, it paws my leg whimpering for a bit of something from ours.

We learn that Antoine is not married (he was engaged to be last winter) and that Thierry, the playful waiter, is. Antoine tells us about the soldier who parachuted into Paris in World War II and slept on a banquette in the restaurant. The soldier now an old man returned recently and told Antoine the story.

Snow is falling across the northern hemisphere, even in Cannes. The *allées* of the Tuileries are packed with hard, Minnesota-like snow. Monet's lyrical panoramas of water lilies at the Musée de l'Orangerie make us forget about the elements for a while. As do the portraits of children painted over the years by French artists, also on exhibit. On the other hand, a tiger's teeth in the neck of a horse seen at the Musée Delacroix yesterday remind one too much of the savage chill.

Our apartment is warm and big and modern. It's on rue de Seine, down the street from La Palette. George Sand once lived in the building, which is undergoing a facelift. Cobblestones are piled in the courtyard, the stucco is fresh, characterless. The spiraling wooden staircase speaks of old charm and perhaps *l'esprit de l'escalier.*

Fellini was one of those people who remembers dreams. He drew and wrote about his in huge notebooks for thirty years. Some of the pages have been reproduced and are being shown, along with excerpts from his films, in a show about the Italian director at the Jeu de Paume.

The colorful caricatures of Fellini with others in comic or disastrous situations are a freewheeling catalog of fears and passions and fantasies. Some focus on his family and Rimini, his birthplace. (He named the four posts of his bed in his grandmother's house after the four movie houses in Rimini.) Others show an adolescent lust for women in the voluptuous style of Anita Ekberg.

The "night work," as he called it, provided fodder for his movies and is every bit as exotic, obsessive, and irrational. The scene of Ekberg and Marcello Mastroianni almost kissing in Trevi Fountain in *La Dolce Vita* plays on a loop in the exhibition. This moment has become embedded in the collective cultural memory, a fact that Fellini, who was treated by a Jungian analyst, would appreciate.

He courted many women, but lived with only one, the actress Giulietta Masina, who starred in his 1954 film *La Strada,* winner of the first Academy Award for a foreign film. He died in 1993, a day after their fiftieth wedding anniversary. She died a few months later.

Madeleine Vionnet put her fingerprint on the labels of her dresses to distinguish them from fakes. She hated knockoffs and fought to develop designers' copyrights. She made simple, beautiful dresses out of four squares of crepe or silk, draped, layered, and sewn in a long column, then wrapped with a sash. Mannequins in the galleries of the Musée des Arts Décoratifs never looked better. Clothed in the revolutionary designer's restrained, muted creations, dating back to the early decades of the 20th century, the mannequins could be mistaken for temple goddesses in ancient Greece.

"She was famous for using the bias cut," Wendy says.

"What is a bias cut?"

"You cut the fabric diagonally against the grain. The fabric follows the form of the body. It moves as the woman moves."

Padding and corsets were not for Madeleine Vionnet. Nor were seams. "The body does not have seams," the designer said, reminding me of Gaudí's statement that there are no straight lines in nature. She started as a seamstress at age eleven and referred to herself as a dressmaker, a technician, disdaining the vagaries of fashion. She used a wooden doll to develop her architectural way with fabric. One did not have to be Marlene Dietrich to wear Vionnet's dresses, though actresses did glamorously. The cut and flow of her gabardine or satin gowns flattered less shapely figures as well.

A stout Russian tries on a slim suit in Etro. He admires himself in a mirror while his children run clamorously around the cases of silk scarves. The nanny and an angry saleswoman wring their hands and hold their tongues.

The maître d' at Café de Flore bends down to look at a man's high heels. The man is dressed in black. His cowboy hat is black. He talks on his cell phone ignoring the less flamboyant men in his entourage.

A hair-tossing girl shares iPod and wine with a skinny boy who has porcelain skin. They laugh and sway in the banquette then abruptly stand up, wrap themselves in scarves, caps, and coats and go outside to smoke. (Sidewalks in Paris are clogged with smokers.) The couple comes back inside and disrobes. The smoking ban allows for more entrances and exits. The ritual of coming and going can be as choreographed as a scene in *Swan Lake.*

Everywhere Parisians peek at cell phones and listen to iPods. They walk down the street, earphones in, talking into space. Wendy and I still like looking at old book covers and landscapes, at the patinas of chairs and chests and other *objets de la réalité.* We look at the chipped-wood-faced bistros painted olive green, aubergine, or midnight blue and through to the dark tables close together. In one, a distinguished man with a glorious aquiline nose leans over a plate of oysters and listens to an artistic-looking woman with what seems like rapture. Maybe's it just the oysters.

We like hearing the church bells, the barges churning up the Seine, the *d'accords* and *à bientôts* on every corner, the warblers in the topiary of the corner garden. We even like the cold if it isn't too cold. Shivering, hearing the gull, the boot on cobblestone, fixes us in a real world, not a synthetic one.

We wait for the movie to start. Our seats are the red of geisha lipstick. On the walls are cranes in the Japanese style lit by serpentine lights. An art-house cinema since the 70s, La Pagode, on rue de Babylone in the 7th, is everybody's favorite discovery in Paris. The elaborate, true-to-form pagoda was the gift of the director of Le Bon Marché to his wife in 1896, around the time the Lumière brothers screened the world's first moving pictures. The first of the ten films the brothers showed, each about fifty seconds long, was *Workers Leaving the Lumière Factory. Bright Star,* the tragic story of John Keats and Fanny Brawne, is playing tonight. It's two hours long.

La Pagode was made into a cinema in the 30s, and after several renovations and the addition of a garden and tearoom, became a protected site. When we come out of the movie house the Eiffel Tower is sparkling madly. La Pagode is just as Parisian in its own intimate way. The little temple's façade is lit, tile roofs swoop, bamboo trees throw shadows in the garden. The neon blue La Pagode sign glows above the door, a door to the world of movies – begun over a century ago when a man cranked perforated film by hand through a projector in a Paris café.

On rue de Seine near our apartment, a man holds open the back door of a glossy, navy blue Citroën. He bows his head. "*Merci beaucoup, Monsieur le Président,*" he says in a hushed voice. A tall man with slicked-back hair slips quickly inside. It's Jacques Chirac. He has come from a gallery on the street. I look in the window. Chirac's tan-brown face is there for a moment looking out. It's a politician's face used to being recognized, and wanting to be.

Adeline wants to start a school. She left her marketing job. "I also started taking singing lessons," she says. Jacques orders a second bottle of wine.

"I hate the 7th," he says with his usual gusto. "Too bourgeois. But I love this restaurant." The food at Christian Constant is rich: quail stuffed with foie gras, fried langoustines. "I'm glad to know you can still enjoy life, David," he says after I tell him about the slight heart attack I had last summer.

We walk across the Esplanade des Invalides past Napoleon's tomb and along rue Saint-Dominique. We pass Basilique Saint-Clotilde behind the National Assembly. "I love walking in Paris at night," Jacques says. "The basilica is beautiful lit up. It reminds me of St. Patrick's in New York. I love New York. All the energy. Paris is so quiet, don't you think?"

How often do you hear a blood-curdling scream on the streets of Paris? Operatic in volume and emotion, it pierces the air and the hearts of all who hear it. We are standing on rue Saint-Honoré across from Hermès. A man holds the woman close. She screams again. We stare, wondering what devastating news she has learned.

Palais
Royal

"Maybe he dumped her," a doughy American woman says flatly to her husband.

Paris stores are often more vibrant than galleries and museums. You marvel at window displays at Astier de Villate, Hermès, Colette, Bonpoint, not to mention arrangements in antique shops and food stores. Behind panes of glass are lavish, whimsical worlds. Inside it's almost as magical. You don't have to buy anything. The French don't. It's the experience. Great lighthearted design is more accessible and more satisfying than a lot of contemporary art.

A walk alone in chilly morning drizzle across the Pont des Arts reminds me of walks in winter across the Stone Arch Bridge in Minneapolis. I walk across the Seine or the Mississippi feeling tired, a little blue. I come back rejuvenated, ready to embrace the day. The sharp, fresh air and the river below winding away to other towns, to other worlds, helps me shed my skin, put on a possible better version of myself.

David arrives with beard and appetite on a rainy Wednesday afternoon. I've lost my appetite after two weeks at Paris tables. Wendy and David go to Aux Lyonnais while I fast at 31 rue de Seine. I catch up with them later at a café. David talks about his new apartment in the West Village, about his work (still mainly arts writing and blogging) and play (courting a girl in a band and going to galleries and parties).

Sarah arrives the next afternoon on an Air France nonstop flight from Los Angeles and joins us in our new apartment on Boulevard Raspail just south of Boulevard Saint-Germain. In a velvet booth at Le Voltaire over roasted *poussin* shared with Wendy (David and I work over a whole roasted duck) she brings us up to date. A costume designer and stylist in L.A., she worked recently on a job for a West Coast cookbook writer. She was just at an "eco resort" with her architect beau and a group of friends from California and New York. Her blonde *boucles* set off her tan.

At Huîtrerie Régis, the tiny oyster restaurant in the 6th, a combination of poor communication (the American) and distracted waiter (the French) leads to platters stacked on our small table holding five dozen oysters. "Oysters for beginner, oysters for main course, oysters for dessert," David says.

"I thought it was a little bizarre," Régis says from behind the counter. He is owner and head oyster shucker. "*Vous aimez des huîtres!*"

Sorry! is the play put on by Footsbarn Theater at Théâtre de l'Épée de Bois in La Cartoucherie. *En famille* we take a long taxi ride to the Bois de Vincennes to see Vincent Gracieux, who has a major role in the production. The play is about the chaos that ensues when a funeral for a composer and a gypsy wedding are booked for the same day.

The circus-like stage covered in sawdust is trod upon by a goat, a chicken, a cat, a tractor, several gypsies riding horses, plus the entire international Footsbarn troop, which includes actors from Bosnia, Holland, Java, England, and France. There's live music, smoke, rain, snow, and bawdy humor. A gorilla plays a flute and glasses of wine are passed around the audience.

Later at La Palette we push together tables for food and wine brought by Alex, Sarah's Portuguese friend who works at the café. "We played at the Globe in London," Vinnie

aprés
le

tells us. "Every actor's dream." He is his charming, laughing self. It's hard to imagine he lived so many years in the U.S. He is even more French with his actor's moustache, if that is possible.

Sarah no longer cares for glitzy nightlife. She's thirty-one. She has dinner with Jerôme and other French friends on a barge. David goes with Piya, a friend from the U.S., to the birthday party of a boy who has "six Belgian brothers." Another night it's a party for *Sang Bleu,* a fashion/art magazine he wrote a piece for. An American artist friend shows up for an exhibition of his paintings. "He didn't seem happy to be there," David says. "He never took off his overcoat."

In our favorite café waiters shake hands and guide us to their tables, especially when Sarah is with us. One whistles like a canary. We smile at the lady cashier. We are packed around the table like chicks in a nest. We order an omelette, a plate of carpaccio, a bottle of Brouilly. We add our voices to the din.

David and Sarah create their own café society, seeing old acquaintances, making new ones. They are linked by text messages, by the pleasure of spending time in Paris, or living here. There's lunch, drinks, a visit to a museum. David talks about one woman he likes: "Then I found out she's a tax lawyer."

A walk with David to the Jardin du Luxembourg, stopping first in a store that carries old books on rue de Vaugirard, across from the garden. Maps of the French provinces in the window caught our eye. From the 1850s, they are drawn elaborately, as if by a precocious child, and are wrapped in faded pink linen boards. They could be from a private collection or from a museum. I am told that yes, they are for sale. I cling tightly to the bag with two of the maps as we cross the street. I feel like I have plundered France's cultural patrimony.

Blue-jacketed guards gather at the gates. It's almost closing time. We make a quick tour, passing the Médici fountain, the basin, the sculptures of French queens, and the Palais du Luxembourg, a dignified, boring building, a perception shaped perhaps by the knowledge that it's where the French senate toils.

Built by Marie de' Medici in the early 17th century, palace and garden were modeled on the Pitti Palace and the Boboli Gardens in Florence, where the young Marie grew up. Exiled from France before it was completed, she never lived in the palace. Members of the German Luftwaffe did though. They commandered it for their Paris residence in World War II.

The gardens are steeped in a kind of serene melancholy in winter. People sit around the basin, crusty with ice. A child sleeps in a stroller. Light-footed women wearing scarves bat a tennis ball back and forth. Men play chess, a few people read on benches. There are no dogs. Never without an air of quiet elegance, the gardens offer sport and solitude, conversation and reverie.

The sharp cold returns on our last day. We fight the wind on Pont Royal as we walk to Restaurant Dalí in the Hôtel Le Meurice. The restaurant is *complet.* We are escorted to the bar, where we order white wine and lunch from the gracious bartender who has worked at the Meurice for thirty years. We look out at the crowd in Le Dalí. Wendy tells again the story of seeing Salvador Dalí and his wife in the hotel.

"Look," Sarah says nodding her head. A woman wearing a long, white fur coat with a white fur hood walks by. She looks like an upright polar bear. Beside her glancing around with equal parts cockiness and self-consciousness is Kanye West.

"That may not beat Salvador," David says. "But it is certainly. . . ."

"Surreal," Wendy and I say together.

"It's more than surreal," he says. "It's fur real."

"If it's fur real," Sarah says, "I'm going to toss a glass of red wine on it."

The last supper. Voltaire's stone face peers through the flowers at the thick pieces of beef on our plates, David's and mine. The ladies are having sole. Sarah tells me again that I should see a therapist and take up yoga. The *entrecôte* reminds her, reminds all of us, of the heart attack I had last summer.

"I first came to Paris fifty years ago," Wendy says.

"How long have we been coming?" Sarah asks.

"Almost thirty years," I say. "Do you remember your first time? You were three and David was six. It was the early eighties."

"We stayed on the Île Saint-Louis."

"When did we stay in Dominique's apartment?"

"That was the second trip in '83."

"I remember climbing up lots of stairs."

"Dad carried you most of the way."

"I remember the bird market."

"I remember the crêpes."

"I remember the cold."

"It was summer the first time. And the second."

Antoine cuts the leftover steak into thin pieces and wraps them in dark green paper. "*Comme un cadeau,*" Sarah says. "David and I will have a nice meal on the plane back to New York. *Merci beaucoup.*"

Antoine tells us about his parents going to the Musée d'Orsay when it was a train station, not a museum, and inviting small groups of hungry Jews who were camped there to come to the restaurant for a meal. "They wrote letters thanking my parents when they got back to their towns and villages," Antoine says.

Sarah and David vanish into the raw night. Wendy and I walk silently along rue de l'Université past the old furniture in windows, past Parisians in shuttered rooms. I pull my scarf up over my chin. A woman peddles by on a bicycle, dog in basket.

"Do you think we will ever have a room of our own in Paris?" I ask.

"I don't think so."

"Why not?"

"You don't want to live here. It wouldn't be the same."

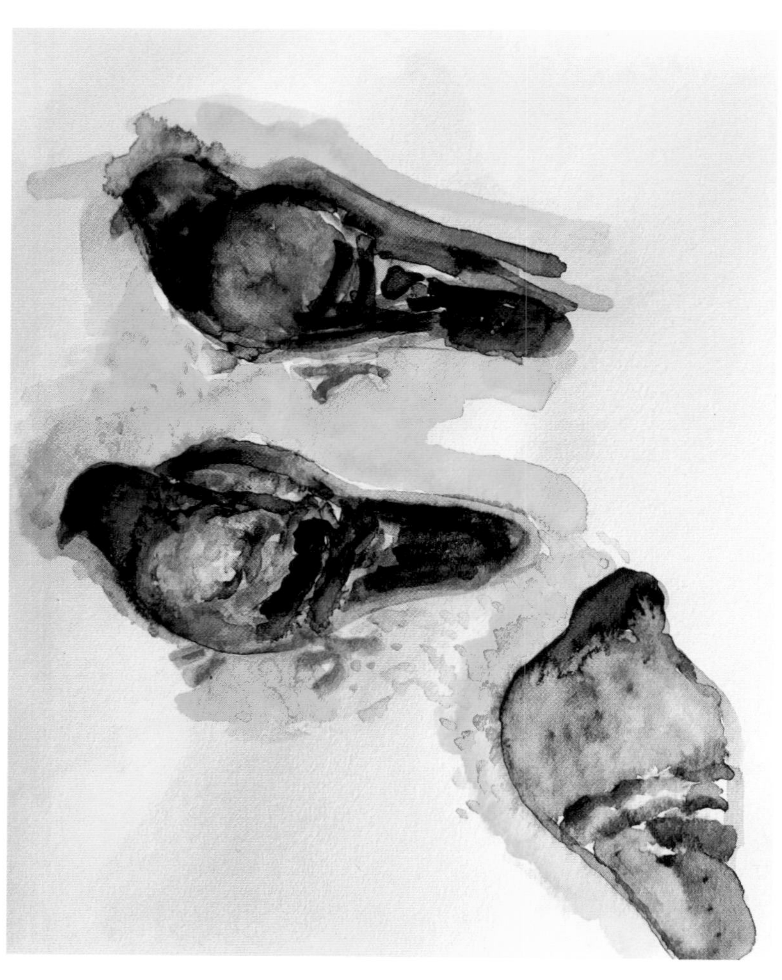

AFTERWORD

I first visited Paris when I was twenty-four. Newly married, my wife and I were living in Holland and during our years there we traveled often to Paris. I was a student, a young writer with artistic aspirations. Wendy was teaching school. Though we were both strongly attracted to Paris, as many Americans are, little did we know the city would become a lifelong passion.

We moved back to America in 1975. Seven years later we returned to Paris, this time with children, ages six and three, in tow. We have been back almost every year since. The city had cast its spell.

After a number of years we began going in winter when tourists were fewer and work at home lightened. David and Sarah, still young, always came with us and pretty soon Paris in winter became a family tradition. Ten days stretched to two weeks, two weeks to three. Now we ring in the New Year in France and don't come home until just before Groundhog Day.

Photographs (and I take plenty of them) have never been enough when I travel. Notebooks full of drawings in watercolors and ink pile up at home and studio. I use watercolors for the same reason Turner did, and Delacroix and Homer and countless amateurs carrying *les carnets de voyage:* a tin of watercolors fits easily into the traveler's bag. They dry fast and impart a fresh, of-the-moment quality to your drawings.

I hoped with brush and color to capture in *Paris in Winter* a bit of the lightness and wit that one finds everywhere in the city. Scottie in Chanel sweater, waiter in white apron having an existential smoke outside his café, umbrella hat on a young woman. I did not lack for subject matter.

Thinking back now from a more mortal age, I think our winters in Paris have become even richer with time, which is not surprising. What is surprising and miraculous to me is to have slipped some part of those lovely ineffable winters between the covers of a book. To have preserved them in a more lasting form. And to be able to share them with others who might find them amusing.

The book starts and ends somewhat arbitrarily. I laid down the brush and fountain pen in 2010. I suppose I stopped because David and Sarah, living busy adult lives, had less time to spend in Paris. But also I think because I had said everything there was to say. The time had come to simply enjoy, not describe. We still go to Paris every winter and usually the kids join us for a while, but now after a day and night of sampling the city's pleasures, I reach for pillow, not notebook.

In the end this is not only a book about Paris but about embracing life. Paris is a city full of life and beauty, which, if you give it a chance, will allow you to embrace it. Better yet, it might embrace you back.

ACKNOWLEDGEMENTS

Special thanks to Wes Del Val at powerHouse Books for adroitly shepherding *Paris in Winter* to publication. I am extremely grateful to editor Will Luckman for his excellent work and to the designers, Kevin Brown of Smart Set, Minneapolis and Krzysztof Poluchowicz at powerHouse, whose skill indelibly shaped the appearance of the book. Many thanks to the talented Megan Wilson who designed the cover. And to Naomi Falk for her expert help in preparing the second edition.

I want to thank Dominique Serrand and his family for opening their doors to us on many visits to France. Our lives have been made richer because of the Serrand family's generosity and grace. Heartfelt thanks to Vincent Gracieux for his warm friendship and to the Hervouets, Jacques and Adeline, for their companionship and bright spirits. I am grateful to the many other friends from America, France, and elsewhere for the happy hours we've shared in Paris.

To my family, Wendy, David, and Sarah, this book is for you with deep love and gratitude. I am especially indebted to my son for his close reading and refining of the manuscript and for his support in finding it a home.

Last, a tip of the hat to the merry men of Le Voltaire—Antoine, Thierry, Pascal, and Régis—for making all the evenings in their restaurant about more than good food.

Paris in Winter

AN ILLUSTRATED MEMOIR

Published in the United States by powerHouse Books,
a division of powerHouse Cultural Entertainment, Inc.
32 Adams Street, Brooklyn, NY 11201-1021

www.powerHouseBooks.com

First edition, 2015
Second edition, 2024

Library of Congress Control Number: 2024936391

ISBN 978-164823-085-1

Printing and binding by Pimlico Book International

Book design by Kevin Brown (Smart Set, Inc.), Krzysztof Poluchowicz (powerHouse Books), and David Coggins

Cover design by Megan Wilson

Type is set in Centaur, originally drawn by Bruce Rogers in 1914 for the Metropolitan Museum of Art. Rogers' primary influence for the Roman was Nicholas Jenson's 1469 Eusebius. Title is Berthold Baskerville, subheadings are Sackers Gothic Heavy.

10 9 8 7 6 5 4 3 2 1

Printed and bound in China